**New Directions for
Teaching and Learning**

Marilla D. Svinicki
EDITOR-IN-CHIEF

R. Eugene Rice
CONSULTING EDITOR

Spirituality in
Higher Education

Sherry L. Hoppe
Bruce W. Speck
EDITORS

Number 104 • Winter 2005
Jossey-Bass
San Francisco

SPIRITUALITY IN HIGHER EDUCATION
Sherry L. Hoppe, Bruce W. Speck (eds.)
New Directions for Teaching and Learning, no. 104
Marilla D. Svinicki, Editor-in-Chief
R. Eugene Rice, Consulting Editor

Microfilm copies of issues and articles are available in 16mm and 35mm, as well as microfiche in 105mm, through University Microfilms Inc., 300 North Zeeb Road, Ann Arbor, Michigan 48106-1346.

NEW DIRECTIONS FOR TEACHING AND LEARNING (ISSN 0271-0633, electronic ISSN 1536-0768) is part of The Jossey-Bass Higher and Adult Education Series and is published quarterly by Wiley Subscription Services, Inc., A Wiley Company, at Jossey-Bass, 989 Market Street, San Francisco, California 94103-1741. Periodicals postage paid at San Francisco, California, and at additional mailing offices. POSTMASTER: Send address changes to New Directions for Teaching and Learning, Jossey-Bass, 989 Market Street, San Francisco, California 94103-1741.

New Directions for Teaching and Learning is indexed in College Student Personnel Abstracts, Contents Pages in Education, and Current Index to Journals in Education (ERIC).

SUBSCRIPTIONS cost $80 for individuals and $170 for institutions, agencies, and libraries. Prices subject to change. See order form at end of book.

EDITORIAL CORRESPONDENCE should be sent to the editor-in-chief, Marilla D. Svinicki, Department of Educational Psychology, University of Texas at Austin, One University Station, D5800, Austin, TX 78712.

www.josseybass.com

CONTENTS

FROM THE SERIES EDITOR

About This Publication. Since 1980, *New Directions for Teaching and Learning (NDTL)* has brought a unique blend of theory, research, and practice to leaders in postsecondary education. *NDTL* sourcebooks strive not only for solid substance but also for timeliness, compactness, and accessibility.

The series has four goals: to inform readers about current and future directions in teaching and learning in postsecondary education, to illuminate the context that shapes these new directions, to illustrate these new directions through examples from real settings, and to propose ways in which these new directions can be incorporated into still other settings.

This publication reflects the view that teaching deserves respect as a high form of scholarship. We believe that significant scholarship is conducted not only by researchers who report results of empirical investigations but also by practitioners who share disciplined reflections about teaching. Contributors to *NDTL* approach questions of teaching and learning as seriously as they approach substantive questions in their own disciplines, and they deal not only with pedagogical issues but also with the intellectual and social context in which these issues arise. Authors deal on the one hand with theory and research and on the other with practice, and they translate from research and theory to practice and back again.

About This Volume. This volume addresses the increased concern over the need for students to develop their spiritual understanding of themselves as well as their intellectual development. For many students, spiritual issues are an important influence on their worldviews and their perspectives on what constitutes truth, which in turn influence their learning, making this an important topic for those who wish to further that learning.

Marilla D. Svinicki
Editor-in-Chief

MARILLA D. SVINICKI is associate professor of educational psychology at the University of Texas at Austin.

EDITORS' NOTES

A recent study on spirituality in higher education by the Higher Education Research Institute, reporting on surveys of 3,680 junior year students and 120,000 entering freshmen at college and universities across the nation, revealed a high percentage of college students place value on integrating spirituality in their lives. Focusing on college students' search for meaning and purpose, the study also discovered a higher-than-expected level of engagement in spiritual and religious pursuits. Despite this clear evidence of student interest, most higher education institutions shy away from actively supporting students in their quest to discover themselves or their reason for being. The project's coprincipal investigators, Alexander and Helen Astin, summarized their assessment of the current state of affairs as a "realization that the relative amount of attention that colleges and universities devote to the 'exterior' and 'interior' aspects of students' development has gotten out of balance. . . . we have increasingly come to neglect the student's inner development—the sphere of values and beliefs, emotional maturity, spirituality, and self-understanding" (Astin and others, 2004, p. 2).

This volume, while not attempting to be a comprehensive guidebook, offers an examination of spirituality in the academy through a number of venues. It begins with a look at myriad definitions of spirituality and also considers legal issues surrounding the inclusion of spirituality in higher education settings. It then examines the importance of the search for truth, provides multiple contexts for spirituality inside and outside the classroom in both sectarian and secular institutions, discusses biological-physiological foundations, offers perspectives on the attributes and effects of spiritual leadership, and closes with cautionary notes.

In Chapter One, Bruce W. Speck recognizes the elusiveness of spirituality but purports that definitions of spirituality can be categorized according to two paradigmatic "worldviews."

John Wesley Lowery in Chapter Two centers a legal analysis of spirituality in higher education on implications of the Constitution's protection of the free exercise of religion and the prohibition against the establishment of religion by the government as set forth by the First Amendment.

In Chapter Three Christina Murphy establishes a historical base for spirituality in higher education and describes the evolution of change through an increasing emphasis on research and business models.

Jennifer Capeheart-Meningall (Chapter Four) expands the discussion by examining how out-of-classroom initiatives can support the search for meaning and interconnectedness, and in Chapter Five, Thomas J. Buttery and Philip S. Roberson probe the biological and physiological foundations of spirituality.

Next, the book offers several perspectives on spirituality in the classroom. First, Miriam Rosalyn Diamond (Chapter Six) describes a book group and its effects on spirituality and teaching. This is followed in Chapter Seven, coauthored by Allen L. Pelletier and John W. McCall, by a look at a modular curriculum that integrates spirituality in teaching health care. In Chapter Eight Harry Lee Poe tenders thoughts on the critical need for sectarian institutions to fill the void created by spirituality avoidance in other institutions. Gary D. Geroy (Chapter Nine) discusses how past spiritual experiences prepare individuals for a growing movement toward workplace spirituality. Last, John Sikula and Andrew Sikula Sr., in Chapter Ten, delineate the connection between service learning and spirituality.

Moving from the classroom to the administrative chambers, in Chapter Eleven Sherry L. Hoppe avows that spirit-filled leaders must integrate the public and private dimensions of their lives, creating wholeness through connectedness of both to the core being.

Daryl V. Gilley closes out the book in Chapter Twelve with cautionary notes about helping others understand who they are and what they may become.

Reference

Astin, A., and others. "Spirituality in Higher Education: A National Study of College Students' Search for Meaning and Purpose." Higher Education Research Institute, University of California, Los Angeles, 2004. http://www.spirituality.ucla.edu/spirituality/reports/FINAL%20EXEC%20SUMMARY.pdf. Accessed Apr. 28, 2004.

Sherry L. Hoppe
Bruce W. Speck
Editors

SHERRY L. HOPPE is president of Austin Peay State University in Clarksville, Tennessee.

BRUCE W. SPECK is provost and vice president for academic and student affairs at Austin Peay State University in Clarksville, Tennessee.

1

Spirituality is difficult to define, but two paradigmatic approaches to worldviews can help provide the basis for two groups of definitions.

What Is Spirituality?

Bruce W. Speck

The question posed in this chapter's title cannot be answered with a consensual definition. In fact, literature on spirituality in higher education offers various definitions. As Palmer (2003) says, "'Spirituality' is an elusive word with a variety of definitions—some compelling, some wifty, some downright dangerous" (p. 377). To investigate spirituality, I provide illustrative definitions, explain three points of tension that help explain divergent definitions, and suggest a way to categorize definitions according to the worldview a definition affirms.

Illustrative Examples

Greenstreet (1999) confirms a lack of consensus in defining spirituality when she says, "There are numerous definitions of the concept of spirituality; these vary in their degree of commonality but do not reflect a consensus of thought" (p. 649). Harlos (2000) calls spirituality an "intractably diffuse and deeply personal concept" (p. 614). Hicks (2003), "based on a reading of some one hundred articles on leadership and workplace spirituality," found a variety of terms were used to define spirituality. "In the abstract, few if any of these terms are objectionable," Hicks notes, "but, as abstractions, they provide little more precision than the word *spirituality* itself does" (p. 55). Like Hicks, others (Johnson, Kristeller, and Sheets, 2004; Laurence, 1999; Lemmer, 2002; Marcic, 2000; Narayanasamy, 1999; Tisdell, 2001), in reviewing literature on spirituality, cite a cacophony of definitions.

The following examples illustrate the definitional dilemma:

• Basically, it [spirituality] is the living out of the organizing story of one's life. In this definition, everyone has a spirituality. The organizing stories of our lives turn around that to which we are ultimately loyal and which we trust for our fulfillment [Bennett, 2003, p. xiii].

• . . . Spirituality is the experience of the transcendent, or the quality of transcendence, something that welcomes, but does not require, religious beliefs [Bento, 2000, p. 653].

• Spirituality is the place in our hearts that holds all of the questions about our purpose in the world and it is reflected in our actions [Campbell, 2003, pp. 20].

• *Spirituality* refers to that noncorporal aspect of each human being that is separate from the mind. *Religion* refers to an organized set of doctrines around faith beliefs within an organization [Clark, 2001, p. 38].

• Spirituality can be understood as the ability to experience connections and to create meaning in one's life [Fried, 2001, p. 268].

• *Spirituality* is the inner experience of the individual when he or she senses a beyond, especially as evidenced by the effect of this experience on his or her behavior when he or she actively attempts to harmonize his or her life with the beyond [Lewis and Geroy, 2000, p. 684].

• By spirituality I mean a sense of compassion, nonviolence, truthfulness, loving kindness, being connected to the whole, and living a simple, peaceful harmonious life [Massoudi, 2003, p. 118].

• Spirituality is the pursuit of a trans-personal and trans-temporal reality that serves as the ontological ground for an ethic of compassion and service [Mayes, 2001, p. 6].

• Spirituality is the eternal human yearning to be connected with something larger than our own egos [Palmer, 2003, p. 377].

Clearly, a consensual definition of spirituality is lacking. To harmonize these definitions would be a herculean task because they point to competing worldviews that are not always fully articulated in the literature, helping explain why the definitions rely on abstractions that, as Hicks (2003) noted, "provide little more precision than the word *spirituality* itself does." We are left with a definitional dilemma.

This dilemma can be explained, in large part, by understanding three points of tension discussed in the literature on spirituality in higher education. How we respond to those three points of tension reveals something about our worldview and shapes the way we define spirituality.

Three Points of Tension

Spirituality, given its large metaphysical sweep, has the potential to posit sundry worldviews, not only because the term itself is an abstraction, open to various interpretations, but also because words with metaphysical import both arise from and inform worldviews. Literature on spirituality in higher education points to at least three points of tension that have helped shape various definitions of spirituality and various worldviews in the United States: separation of church and state, the reigning epistemology of higher education, and lack of faculty education in addressing spirituality.

Separation of Church and State. Despite the seemingly absolute barrier that the word *separation* implies in the phrase "separation of church and state," such is not the case. The Founders never intended to exclude or separate religion from the state; rather, they neither wanted to privilege a particular religious perspective nor to exclude secular perspectives (Mayes, 2001). Thus, the Founders were opposed to establishing a state-endorsed religious perspective and to not allowing freedom of dissent from a secular viewpoint. This attempt to balance competing interests is, of course, a continual walk on a tightrope. The high-wire juggling is complicated because "The authors of the Constitution and the Bill of Rights laid a framework to maintain the legal nonestablishment of religion, but they still assumed an effective cultural establishment of Christianity" (Hicks, 2003, p. 65). When the balancing act tilts toward religious expression, those fearful of the influence of religion on constitutional liberties attempt to redress the balance and vice versa. Marcic (2000) captures the uneasiness of this tension by referring to the obvious "squeamishness . . . in many people when the words *religion* and *God* are used" (p. 629). A like uneasiness accompanies the rhetoric of those who see the culture tilting toward an unabashed endorsement of secularism. Even highly regarded Justice Sandra Day O'Connor acknowledges the difficulty of separating religion from the government: "Speaking broadly about ceremonial prayer and symbols allowed in government buildings, she said, 'It's so hard to draw the line'" (Biskupic, 2005, 2A).

In public higher education, the supposed wall between church and state and the attendant confusion that issues from that misleading metaphor can create a chilling effect, what Lee, Matzkin, and Arthur (2004) describe as "fears of imposing one's so-called 'personal views,' violating laws regarding the separation of church and state." Such fears help explain why "educators have refrained from incorporating religion and spirituality into the[ir] institution[s]" (no page number). Indeed, Collins, Hurst, and Jacobson (1987) say, "The principle of separation of church and state has become so engrained that people say those words and diffuse any interest in the topics of spirituality and religion when nothing needs to be diffused" (p. 275). According to Palmer (2003), students are taught long before they enter academe to resist any questions concerning spiritual issues: ". . . . Our students are told from an early age that school is not the place to bring their questions of meaning: take them home, to your religious community, or to your therapist, but do not bring them to school. So students learn, as a matter of survival, to keep their hearts hidden when in the groves of academe" (p. 379). In short, "Religious and spiritual inquiries are not considered to be intellectual endeavors; consequently, they receive little respect and attention in the academy" (Raper, 2001, p. 15).

The definitional dilemma merely adds confusion to an already chilling silence concerning the role of higher education in addressing the relationship between learning, teaching, religion, and spirituality. Indeed, critical terms are blurred, in part, "because of the fuzziness in the distinctions we draw between religion and spirituality" (Fried, 2001, p. 263). Part of the reason for that fuzziness can be attributed to an attempt to solve the separation problem by divorcing spirituality from religion. Thus, literature on spirituality in higher education regularly repeats the refrain "spirituality is not religion." But to make that stratagem work, spirituality is often defined in terms of personal commitment to "something." However, personal commitment does not exactly fit the definitional bill because the *telos* of spirituality, according to those who subscribe to personal commitment to something, cannot result in that something being merely individual fulfillment. A larger goal—generally a goal that encompasses the good of the social order—is introduced to rescue personal spiritual commitment from narcissism. Once rescued, however, the difference between social actions or even personal ethical conduct grounded in spirituality is extremely difficult to distinguish from the social actions or personal ethical conduct many religious people endorse. Little wonder that distinctions between spirituality and religion, despite the refrain that the two are separate, appear to be hazy at best.

Reigning Epistemology of Higher Education. This definitional dilemma is further exacerbated by what Chickering calls "unleavened doses of objectivity and empirical rationality" (2003, p. 41) in higher education. In fact, "Our overwhelming valuation of rational empiricism—a conception of truth as objective and external—and of knowledge as a commodity de-legitimizes active public discussions of purpose and meaning, authenticity and identity, or spirituality and spiritual growth" (Chickering, 2003, p. 44). Palmer (1987) calls objectivism in higher education a "seemingly bloodless epistemology" (p. 22). Elsewhere, Palmer (2003) notes that "the bright light of science has been almost exclusively focused on 'objective realities' such as technique, curricula, and cash, rather than on soulful factors such as relational trust" (p. 385). Thus, "the exploration of faith," according to Raper (2001), is seen "as anti-intellectual and politically risky" (p. 21).

As with the separation-between-church-and-state tension, the epistemological tension produces a chilling effect. For example, Zajonc (2003) believes that "formidable barriers block the integration of contemplation and spirituality into higher education" and notes that "the institutional barriers that do exist are mostly informal and take the form of academic peer pressure to eschew approaches involving spiritual or even moral and philosophical analysis [sic] of the disciplines. We should not underestimate the powerful effect this pressure has on the open exploration of important issues within the disciplines, especially by junior faculty. This is all the more ironic, and even tragic, because the academy ostensibly commits itself to completely open inquiry, yet quietly dismisses at the outset certain domains or methodologies as out-of-bounds" (p. 53).

In effect, the "seemingly bloodless epistemology" of higher education prohibits open, frank discussion of spirituality or religion unless, of course, those topics can be shoehorned into the premises of naturalism. Attempts at such shoehorning in literature on spirituality in higher education try to make the concept fit by appealing to personal beliefs. Under the bloodless epistemology, spirituality is tolerated as long as it remains a private concern. As Lindholm (2004) points out, ". . . the structure and culture of academia [have] encouraged faculty to act as if their most deeply held values and beliefs are irrelevant to their work" (p. 13). That is, deeply held values and beliefs that challenge the bloodless epistemology must be kept private and not intrude on serious academic work. Mayes (2001) concurs, citing scholarship that shows a "rather high degree of religious commitment among American scholars, [yet] many of them find that academic culture has constructed a variety of explicit and also tacit constraints against including these commitments in their scholarship." That such constraints "constitute a violation of the very concept of pluralism, which so many of us hold so dear in academic culture" (p. 14) appears to be just another irony of academic life that persists with little regard for its deleterious effect on academic freedom—and integrity.

This irony, however, is parallel to the definitional dilemma produced by the privatization of spirituality under the chilling effect of the separation of church and state. Again, religion has to be greatly marginalized or dismissed to make way for privatized spirituality. Thus, academics may not see themselves as religious but may identify themselves as spiritual. As Johnson, Kristeller, and Sheets (2004) point out, ". . . many social scientists and academics in general show a trend toward dichotomizing or polarizing religion and spirituality; that is, viewing them as opposites. This polarization is accompanied by a tendency to characterize spirituality as good, individualistic, liberating, and mature, while portraying religion as bad, institutionalized, constraining, and childish" (p. 3).

Spirituality, now liberated from religion, needs further to be liberated from the supernatural, a hallmark of religion. Thus, it is not surprising that "the exact role of the supernatural in defining spirituality has been a point of debate, with some authors arguing that a concept of the sacred is essential in defining spirituality . . . while others argue that spirituality can be completely atheistic and separate from any organized religious context" (Johnson, Kristeller, and Sheets, 2004, p. 3). That debate in academe is tilting heavily toward a nonsupernatural point of view, yet a point of view that can include "God terms," if the terms are inclusive. For example, Burrows (2001) affirms, "There is generally a sense of acceptance that God is acknowledged and defined by different individuals and groups in many ways such as the Higher Power, Buddha, Allah, the Force, or the Spirit of the Universe" (pp. 138–139). *God,* Burrows says, is a perfectly acceptable term if by using the term a person means a plurality of names that are assumed to point either to the same entity in the natural realm or to a personal idea divorced from the supernatural. It appears to be of little moment that many of those who bow to Allah, for example, find reprehensible bowing the knee to Buddha—and find it impossible to divorce Allah from a supernatural realm.

Tolerance and diversity are often cited to justify the nonsupernatural view of spirituality that, nonetheless, may be laced with terms carrying metaphysical freight. In the process of trying to separate spirituality from both religion and the supernatural, to ensure that spirituality is a matter of one's heart, individualism is affirmed. But because individualism can become narcissistic, spirituality must be directed toward the social good, if the academy is going to take this private concern with any seriousness.

Palmer (2003) provides a synthesis of the various points of epistemological tension when he concludes, "*What* one names this core of the human being is of no real consequence to me, because no one can claim to know its true name. But *that* one names it is, I believe, crucial. For 'it' is the ontological reality of being human that keeps us from regarding ourselves, our colleagues, or our students as raw material to be molded into whatever form serves the reigning economic or political regime" (pp. 377–378). There's little reason to debate what "it" is, as long as it serves the social good of promoting human dignity. To argue against this noble goal would be to betray humanity. But it remains, ironically, in Palmer's own words, "an elusive word with a variety of definitions" (2003, p. 377) and does not appear to help solve the definitional dilemma.

Lack of Faculty Education in Addressing Spirituality. Because of confusion about the constitutional issues regarding the role of spirituality in higher education and a dominating epistemology that brooks no meaningful discussion about spirituality unless, perhaps, spirituality is a private good, it is little wonder that faculty are unprepared to address what constitutes spirituality when the topic emerges during the educational enterprise. If spirituality is a legitimate academic concern, faculty should be provided insights into addressing the topic with students. Even in disciplines that could make a legitimate claim to helping students address the spiritual needs their future clients or patients will raise, faculty education in spirituality is virtually absent and absent again from the faculty's classrooms.

For example, "Few counselors are exposed to spirituality during their training . . . thus, they risk alienating clients who present with spiritual issues, particularly if the counselor is unaware of his or her own spirituality" (Souza, 2002, p. 213). In addition, "Many studies have highlighted the concern as to whether nurses are prepared to provide spiritual care" (Lemmer, 2002, p. 482). Pesut (2002), in speaking about obstacles to preparing nurses for caring for patients' spiritual needs, notes, "Barriers to integrating spiritual care into the curriculum may include the complexity of defining the concept within a multicultural society; the culture we live in that values secularism and materialism; the resource limitations experienced by many nursing programs; and the lack of models, faculty preparedness, and accountability" (p. 129). In short, ". . . there has been little thoughtful public recognition by faculty that this concern [supporting students' development of personal and spiritual values] should be addressed as part of their roles and responsibilities" (Stamm, 2003, p. 8).

Related issues, such as proselytizing students (Johnson, Kristeller, and Sheets, 2004; Lindholm, 2004; Mayes, 2001) and addressing students' concerns about their privacy regarding spirituality (Johnson and Mutschelknaus, 2001) are difficult to resolve if spirituality has no legitimate place in the curriculum. In fact, even designing faculty development opportunities requires not only acceptance of spirituality as an appropriate topic for academic discourse but also a narrowing of the definitions of spirituality.

Responding to the Points of Tension: Toward Consensual Definitions of Spirituality

Foundational to any definition of spirituality is the worldview from which the definition arises. Unfortunately, definitions of spirituality, even including the language in texts in which they are embedded, are often not attended by cogent statements that explain a scholar's worldview. Hints of what a scholar's worldview might be are suggestive at best, but worldviews, because they purport to provide a cohesive framework for understanding what exists, by necessity need to address seminal concerns. I suggest three concerns a worldview must address: what exists?, who or what is in charge?, and what is the purpose of existence? A great deal of the definitional dilemma can be solved by applying these three concerns to definitions of spirituality.

What Exists? To answer the question of what exists, two possibilities have to be entertained: the possibility of natural existence only and the possibility of natural and supernatural existence. I recognize that this is a simplistic approach to complex philosophical concepts, but for my present purpose, this rough categorization will do.

One possibility is that all that exists is the natural world, what Sagan (1980) calls the cosmos. If that is the case, spirituality must be defined in terms of the natural order. According to this worldview, no supernatural order exists, and therefore, the natural order is a closed system. Fried (2001) seems to endorse this naturalistic worldview by saying, "We need to discuss spirituality not because God exists, but because we exist and we need to create meaning for ourselves" (p. 277). An implication of Fried's statement is that recourse to a supernatural order that would provide meaning is not possible.

The other possible way to understand what exists is to posit both a natural and a supernatural realm. The details of the relationship between these two realms vary given particular philosophical or theological traditions, but in virtually all cases, the supernatural realm is ontologically primary. Thus, the natural realm exists because it is derived from and sustained by the supernatural realm.

Who or What Is in Charge? In a naturalistic worldview, who or what is in charge can be answered only by referring to "natural" forces, whether nature or humans or a combination of both. Evolution is typically evoked as the force that causes the cosmos to change. Generally in the literature on spirituality in higher education, humans are the focal point of authority. In fact, "what particularly marks modern spirituality is its tendency toward individual interpretation and idiosyncratic experience" (Mayes, 2001, p. 12). Like Fried, Mayes locates authority in the individual. Individuals have the authority—the right, the responsibility, and the power—to make meaning. The problem of contested authority is difficult to solve when authority is vested in individuals *qua* individuals. The bumper sticker "Question Authority!" is a succinct (albeit undoubtedly unintended) statement of the dilemma of contested authority.

The question of authority when a supernatural realm exists is answered by appealing to the ontological primacy of the supernatural realm. The dependency of the natural realm on the supernatural realm is evidence of the ultimate authority vested in the supernatural realm. This does not mean that people do not have authority of various sorts, but their authority is derivative, and they are accountable to the supernatural realm, whether, for example, that accountability is a last judgment or reincarnation. In sum, "Spirituality may be thought of as being primarily unique to the individual and purely personal, or it may be conceived as having an external referent and normative basis for understanding spiritual truth" (Daniels, Franz, and Wong, 2000, p. 544).

What Is the Purpose of Existence? The question about purpose, under naturalistic presuppositions, cannot include an afterlife, so whatever counts for purpose only counts in relation to the natural order. Under naturalistic worldviews, ethics takes on high importance because how a person relates to the natural order is paramount. Dalton (2001), for example, stresses the ethical dimension of individual spirituality by saying,

> A spiritual quest that focuses primarily on self-definition and self-understanding fails to consider equally serious concerns about relationships with others and the search for transcendence that are central to that quest. If spirituality is regarded as essentially a private and introspective process, a kind of private journey of the soul, in which few if any moral claims are made upon the spiritual traveler, then the claim of spirituality as feel-goodness has some validity. . . . but I think we fail as educators if we do not help students link the ethical claims of life and work with others to one's relationship with what is transcendent and sacred [p. 23].

I take it that Dalton is not using the terms *soul, transcendent,* and *sacred* as pointing to a supernatural realm. However, by using such terms, Dalton introduces confusion about how his concept of spirituality should be understood. Indeed, the introduction of "God terms" to describe natu-ralistic worldviews creates confusion. For instance, when a person who espouses a naturalistic worldview uses terms like *sacred, spirit, God, tran-scendence,* and *spirituality,* the person is not speaking about a supernatural or transcendent order above or over the natural order. Yet, these terms, quite naturally, point to such an order. To qualify spirit as "the vital prin-ciple or animating force within living beings; that which constitutes one's unseen intangible being; the real sense or significance of something" (Scott, 1994, p. 64) is apt if no supernatural realm is in view. A definition of spir-ituality issuing from that definition of spirit should include a clear state-ment that confines spirituality to the natural order. It is helpful to acknowledge that "spirituality is often connected to things like meaning in life, which can be an entirely secular affair, or meditation, which can also be divorced from any specific religious context" (Johnson, Kristeller, and Sheets, 2004, p. 3). Indeed, definitions of spirituality grounded in a natu-ralistic worldview should be carefully crafted so that they cannot in good faith be misconstrued as allowing a realm beyond the natural.

The same principle holds true for definitions about spirituality grounded in a natural-supernatural worldview. Definitions that acknowl-edge the validity of a dualistic worldview should not fudge on either side of the dualism to minimize the other side. "Thus, spirituality is conceptual-ized as having vertical and horizontal dimensions. The vertical dimension reflects the relationship to God or a supreme being. The horizontal dimen-sion reflects both our connectedness to others and nature, and to our intra-personal connectedness . . . " (Pesut, 2002, p. 128). As Hicks (2003) warns, "Attempts to translate religiously particular values into common spiritual or secular values are reductionistic at best and inaccurate at worst" (p. 165), a warning that adherents to both worldviews should heed.

Conclusion

In suggesting that definitional dilemmas are rife in the literature on spiritu-ality in higher education, I could be accused of stating the obvious. Unfortunately, the definitional dilemmas tend to undercut the obvious by appealing to tolerance and diversity, hallowed concepts today in the acad-emy, that suggest unanimity is normative. By invoking these concepts, some scholars, it appears, want to erase difficulties that call into question their notions of tolerance and diversity. I assume such attempts to erase differ-ences to establish tolerance and diversity are done with the best of intentions, but in any case the attempts are based on naïve notions of commonality. Hicks (2003) drives this point home when he says, ". . . the claim that 'spir-ituality creates common ground' cannot be readily established without undertaking more work at least to address the philosophical and theological difficulties of the term and its definitional components. Authors who make broad and sweeping claims about spirituality should clarify the connections and coherence of their account" (p. 56).

Proponents of spirituality as a legitimate academic subject are asking too much of colleagues who are not warm to such a proposal if they cannot at least provide a coherent definition of spirituality grounded in an explicit, cogent worldview as the focal point of an academic dialogue. I have outlined an approach that provides guidance as we seek to solve the definitional dilemma. It may be that no consensual definition can be fashioned, given the two paradigmatic worldviews I have posited, but it should be the case that definitions of spirituality make explicit the presuppositions on which they are based, providing at least two distinct groups of definitions under the aegis of two paradigmatic worldviews.

References

Bennett, J. B. *Academic Life: Hospitality, Ethics, and Spirituality*. Bolton, Mass.: Anker, 2003.

Bento, R. F. "The Little Inn at the Crossroads: A Spiritual Approach to the Design of a Leadership Course." *Journal of Management Education,* 2000, 24(5), 650–661.

Biskupic, J. "Commandments Cases May Hinge on 1 High Court Justice." *USA Today,* March 5, 2005, p. 2A.

Burrows, L. T. "Dancing on the Edge." In V. M. Miller, and M. M. Ryan (eds.), *Transforming Campus Life: Reflections on Spirituality and Religious Pluralism*. New York: Lang, 2001.

Campbell, L. H. "The Spiritual Lives of Artists/Teachers." Paper presented at the Annual Meeting of the American Educational Research Association, Chicago, April 21–25, 2003.

Chickering, A. W. "Reclaiming Our Soul." *Change,* 2003, Jan./Feb., pp. 39–45.

Clark, R. T. "The Law and Spirituality: How the Law Supports and Limits Expression of Spirituality on the College Campus." In M. A. Jablonski (ed.), *The Implications of Student Spirituality for Student Affairs Practice*. New Directions for Student Services, no. 95. San Francisco: Jossey-Bass, 2001.

Collins, J. R., Hurst, J. C., and Jacobson, J. K. "The Blind Spot Extended: Spirituality." *Journal of College Student Personnel,* 1987, 28(3), 274–276.

Dalton, J. C. "Career and Calling: Finding a Place for the Spirit in Work and Community." In M. A. Jablonski (ed.), *The Implication of Student Spirituality for Student Affairs Practice*. New Directions for Student Services, no. 95. San Francisco: Jossey-Bass, 2001.

Daniels, D., Franz, R. S., and Wong, K. "A Classroom with a Worldview: Making Spiritual Assumptions Explicit in Management Education." *Journal of Management Education,* 2000, 24(5), 540–561.

Fried, J. "Civility and Spirituality." In V. M. Miller, and M. M. Ryan (eds.), *Transforming Campus Life: Reflections on Spirituality and Religious Pluralism*. New York: Lang, 2001.

Greenstreet, W. M. "Teaching Spirituality in Nursing: A Literature Review." *Nurse Education Today,* 1999, 19, 649–658.

Harlos, K. P. "Toward a Spiritual Pedagogy: Meaning, Practice, and Applications in Management Education." *Journal of Management Education,* 2000, 24(5), 612–627.

Hicks, D. A. *Religion and the Workplace: Pluralism, Spirituality, Leadership*. New York: Cambridge, 2003.

Johnson, P., and Mutschelknaus, M. "Disembodied Spirituality: Conflicts in the Writing Center." Paper presented at the Annual Meeting of the Conference on College Composition and Communication, Denver, Mar. 14–17, 2001.

Johnson, T. J., Kristeller, J., and Sheets, V. L. "Religiousness and Spirituality in College Students: Separate Dimension with Unique and Common Correlates." *Journal of*

College and Character, 2005, *1,* 1–36 [e-journal]. http://www.collegevalues.org/pdfs/Johnson.pdf. Accessed Sept. 20, 2004.

Laurence, P. "Can Religion and Spirituality Find a Place in Higher Education?" *About Campus,* 1999, *4*(5), 11–16.

Lee, J. J., Matzkin, A., and Arthur, S. "Understanding Students' Religious and Spiritual Pursuits: A Case Study at New York University." *Journal of College and Character,* 2004, *1,* 1–33 [e-journal]. http://www.collegevalues.org/pdfs/Lee2.pdf. Accessed Sept. 20, 2004.

Lemmer, C. "Teaching the Spiritual Dimension of Nursing Care: A Survey of U.S. Baccalaureate Nursing Programs." *Journal of Nursing Education,* 2002, *41*(11), 482–490.

Lewis, J. S., and Geroy, G. D. "Employee Spirituality in the Workplace: A Cross-Cultural View for the Management of Spiritual Employees." *Journal of Management Education,* 2000, *24*(5), 682–694.

Lindholm, J. "The Role of Faculty in College Students' Spirituality." *Journal of College and Character,* 2004, *1,* no page nos. [e-journal]. http://www.collegevalues.org/articles.cfm?id=1221&a=1. Accessed Sept. 20, 2004.

Marcic, D. "God, Faith, and Management Education." *Journal of Management Education,* 2000, *24*(5), 628–649.

Massoudi, M. "Can Scientific Writing Be Creative?" *Journal of Science Education and Technology,* 2003, *12*(2), 115–128.

Mayes, C. "Cultivating Spiritual Reflectivity in Teachers." *Teacher Education Quarterly,* 2001, *28*(2), 5–22.

Narayanasamy, A. "ASSET: A Model for Actioning Spirituality and Spiritual Care Education and Training in Nursing." *Nurse Education Today,* 1999, *19*(4), 274–285.

Palmer, P. "Community, Conflict, and Ways of Knowing: Ways to Deepen Our Educational Agenda." *Change,* 1987, *19*(5), 20–25.

Palmer, P. J. "Teaching with Heart and Soul: Reflections on Spirituality in Teacher Education." *Journal of Teacher Education,* 2003, *54*(5), 376–385.

Pesut, B. "The Development of Nursing Students' Spirituality and Spiritual Care-Giving." *Nurse Education Today,* 2002, *22,* 128–135.

Raper, J. "'Losing Our Religion': Are Students Struggling in Silence?" In V. M. Miller, and M. M. Ryan (eds.), *Transforming Campus Life: Reflections on Spirituality and Religious Pluralism.* New York: Lang, 2001.

Sagan, C. *Cosmos.* New York: Random House, 1980.

Scott, K. T. "Leadership and Spirituality: A Quest for Reconciliation." In J. A. Conger and Associates (eds.), *Spirit at Work: Discovering Spirituality in Leadership.* San Francisco: Jossey-Bass, 1994.

Souza, K. Z. "Spirituality in Counseling: What Do Counseling Students Think about It?" *Counseling and Values,* 2002, *46,* 213–217.

Stamm, L. "Can We Bring Spirituality Back to Campus? Higher Education's Re-Engagement with Values and Spirituality." *Journal of College and Character,* 2003, no page nos. [e-journal]. http://www.collegevalues.org/articles.cfm?a=1&id=1075. Accessed Sept. 20, 2004.

Tisdell, E. J. "Spirituality in Adult and Higher Education." Washington, D.C.: Office of Educational Research and Improvement, 2001. (ED 459 370)

Zajonc, A. "Spirituality in Higher Education: Overcoming the Divide." *Liberal Education,* 2003 Winter, pp. 50–58.

BRUCE W. SPECK *is provost and vice president for academic and student affairs at Austin Peay State University in Clarksville, Tennessee.*

2

*An increasingly litigious environment, combined with a
renewed interest in spirituality, makes it imperative for
higher education officials to be cognizant of the legal
implication of two competing fundamental rights.*

What Higher Education Law Says About Spirituality

John Wesley Lowery

Of the more vexing topics that institutions of higher education, particularly
public colleges and universities, must resolve when seeking to more effectively address spirituality in and outside of the classroom are legal issues.
O'Neil (1997) warned, "Religious expression on the public campus has been
persistently troublesome and may become more so" (p. xv). Clark (2001)
observed that many on campus were hesitant to address spirituality because
they were "unaware of or confused about the legal issues involved in religion
and spirituality on the college campus" (p. 38). This confusion is born in
part from the two seemingly conflicting clauses of the First Amendment that
address issues of religion: the Establishment Clause and the Free Exercise
Clause. Kaplin and Lee (1995) described the requirements under the Establishment Clause for public institutions of higher education, "Under the
Establishment Clause of the First Amendment, public institutions must
maintain a neutral stance regarding religious beliefs and activities; they must,
in other words, maintain religious neutrality. Public institutions cannot favor
or support one religion over another, and they cannot favor or support religion over nonreligion" (p. 56). Conversely, institutions of higher education
also cannot favor or support nonreligion over religion (Lowery, 2004).

General Principles

To understand the appropriate place of spirituality in higher education
today, it is important to consider the Constitution's protection of the free
exercise of religion and prohibition against the establishment of religion by
the government as set forth in the First Amendment (Lowery, 2000, 2004).

The courts are often forced to balance these two competing fundamental rights against one another in deciding cases involving education. In *Lemon* v. *Kurtzman* (1971) and *Tilton* v. *Richardson* (1971), the Supreme Court established a three-pronged test for determining whether a governmental program violates the establishment of religion clause of the First Amendment. In *Lemon,* the court ruled that policies or laws need not create an official state religion to violate the First Amendment, stating, "A given law might not establish a state religion, but nevertheless be one 'respecting' that end in the sense of being a step that could lead to such establishment, and hence offend the First Amendment" (403 U.S. 611). Drawing on earlier rulings, the Supreme Court in *Lemon* articulated its new three-pronged test: "First, the statute must have a secular legislative purpose; second, its principal or primary effect must be one that neither advances nor inhibits religion; finally, the statute must not foster 'an excessive government entanglement with religion'" [citations omitted] (403 U.S. 612–613 [1971]).

Kaplin and Lee (1995) acknowledged that while the first prong of the *Lemon* (1971) test was relatively easy to understand, "the other two prongs (effect and entanglement) have been both very important and very difficult to apply in particular cases" (p. 59). Chief Justice Burger noted in his ruling in *Tilton* (1971), "Candor compels the acknowledgment that we can only dimly perceive the boundaries of permissible government activity in this sensitive area of constitutional adjudication" (403 U.S. 678).

Most cases in which the Supreme Court has addressed the free exercise of religion in an educational context have originated in the K-12 setting. One of the earliest cases in which the court addressed this important question was *West Virginia Board of Education* v. *Barnette* (1943). The Supreme Court overturned a West Virginia policy requiring students to salute the American flag, which violated Jehovah's Witnesses' religious beliefs. Justice Jackson wrote, "If there is any fixed star in our constitutional constellation, it is that no official, high or petty, can prescribe what will be orthodox, in politics, nationalism, religion, or other matters of opinion or force citizens to confess by word or act their faith therein" (319 U.S. 642). In *Employment Division, Department of Human Resources of Oregon* v. *Smith* (1990), the court refined its test (*Sherbert* v. *Verner,* 1963; *Wisconsin* v. *Yoder,* 1972) for determining if government regulation affecting religious practice violated the Free Exercise of Religion Clause of the Constitution. The court instead allowed "a neutral, generally applicable regulatory law that compelled activity forbidden by an individual's religion" (494 U.S. 880).

The Supreme Court's most recent balancing of these two competing clauses of the First Amendment involving higher education was *Locke* v. *Davey* (2004). The court upheld a Washington State scholarship program, the Promise Scholarship, that prohibited students pursuing a degree in theology from receiving the scholarship. Joshua Davey was a student who had received a Promise Scholarship but learned that he could not use the scholarship if he pursued his desired degree in pastoral ministries at Northwest College. He sued, claiming that the restrictions on the Promise Scholarship violated the Free Exercise and Establishment clauses. Chief Justice Rehnquist, writing for the majority concluded, "The State's interest in not funding the pursuit of devotional degrees is substantial and the exclusion of such funding places a relatively minor burden on Promise Scholars. If any room exists between the two Religion Clauses, it must be here" (540 U.S. 1315).

Prayer at Graduation and Other Public Events

One of the most visible and confusing aspects of spirituality and religion on public college campuses involves prayers or invocations at graduation and other public events on campus. Part of this confusion stems from the Supreme Court's own rulings in this area. The Supreme Court has consistently ruled that prayers at public events such as graduation or football games are unconstitutional in the context of K-12 public education, even when led by students (*Engel* v. *Vitale,* 1962; *Lee* v. *Weisman,* 1992; *Santa Fe Independent School District* v. *Doe,* 2000; *School District of Abington Township* v. *Schempp,* 1963; *Wallace* v. *Jaffree,* 1985). In its school prayer cases, the Supreme Court has stressed the coercive nature of prayer in the public school context even while acknowledging that participation in some events was not purely mandatory. In *Lee* v. *Weisman* (1992), the court warned, "the Constitution guarantees that government may not coerce anyone to support or participate in religion or its exercise" (505 U.S. 587).

The Supreme Court has not, however, heard a case involving prayer in public higher education. Generally, the appellate courts have distinguished between higher education and the K-12 setting and reached a different conclusion from the one suggested by the Supreme Court's rulings in the K-12 setting. In both *Tanford* v. *Brand* (1997) and *Chaudhuri* v. *Tennessee* (1997), the courts of appeals for the Seventh and Sixth Circuits, respectively, upheld as constitutional religious invocations at the graduations of Indiana University and Tennessee State University. A primary factor in each court's analysis was the absence of the coercive environment described by the Supreme Court in its rulings. In *Chaudhuri,* the court also stressed the absence of any likely influence of prayers on the graduates, unlike the impressionable nature of school-aged students. The one exception to this trend is the Court of Appeals for the Fourth Circuit's ruling in *Mellen* v. *Bunting* (2003). The court ruled that General Bunting, then superintendent of Virginia Military Institution (VMI), had violated the Constitution in reinstating the tradition of supper prayer in 1995. The case's implications are severely limited by the unique environment at VMI, described as highly coercive, that is unlikely to be found at other public institutions. The Commonwealth of Virginia appealed the case to the U.S. Supreme Court, which declined to hear the case. In an unusual move, two justices wrote opposing opinions regarding their views on whether the court should hear the case (Klein, 2004). Justice Scalia argued that the court should have taken up the case because of the "weighty questions" involved and his concerns regarding application of the court's rulings from K-12 education to colleges and universities.

Spirituality in the Classroom

Over the past several years, legal conflicts have arisen on several public college campuses resulting from disconnects between students' religious beliefs and academic requirements or activities of the institution. These cases illustrate the effect of both students' and faculty members' religious beliefs on spirituality in the classroom.

In *Axson-Flynn* v. *Johnson* (2004), the Court of Appeals for the Tenth Circuit considered the case of Christina Axson-Flynn. Axson-Flynn was a devout Mormon and a student in the University of Utah's Actor Training Program (ATP). During her first semester in the program, she refused to take God's name in vain or say "fuck" during classroom acting exercises. She was instructed by the ATP faculty to "'get over' her refusal to use those words, saying that not using the words would stunt her growth as an actor" (356 F.3d 1280). Axson-Flynn withdrew on her own from the acting program after her second semester, believing that eventually she would be forced to leave the program by the ATP faculty. She brought suit under Section 1983 of Title 42 of the U.S. Code in federal district court. Her suit was dismissed by that court, and she appealed the decision to the Court of Appeals for the Tenth Circuit. She claimed that forcing her to use the words in question violated her rights under the First Amendment to both freedom of speech and the free exercise of religion. The court observed in analyzing her free speech claims, "That schools must be empowered at times to restrict the speech of their students for pedagogical purposes is not a controversial proposition. By no means is such power limited to the very basic level of a teacher's ability to penalize a student for disruptive classroom behavior" (356 F.3d 1291). Similarly, in *Settle* v. *Dickson County School Board* (1995), the Sixth Circuit upheld the right of a ninth-grade teacher to prohibit a student from writing her research paper on Jesus Christ because of the educational goals of the assignment. However, the court also considered whether the requirement that Axson-Flynn use words that she believed violated her Mormon beliefs was truly born out of an educational goal or pedagogical concern or instead simply a pretext to punish her for her religious beliefs. The court did not resolve this issue but remanded the case for further consideration. The court also remanded the issue of her Free Exercise claims for further consideration by the district court but placed greater emphasis on her free speech claims. Brown (2002) noted that in recent years in cases involving both freedom of speech and free exercise of religion claims that plaintiffs had greater success under former penumbra of rights. After the Court of Appeals for the Tenth Circuit ruled in this case, the University of Utah settled Axson-Flynn's case by agreeing to appoint a committee to develop a policy on religious accommodation.

The other case that garnered considerable public attention involved the University of North Carolina (UNC) at Chapel Hill's decision to assign a portion of Michael Sells' *Approaching the Qur'an: The Early Revelations* (1999) as part of the institution's 2002 summer orientation reading program (*Yacovelli* v. *Moeser,* 2004). Several groups originally attempted to block the reading program entirely, claiming that the program violated the Establishment Clause of the First Amendment, but the federal district court and the Court of Appeals for the Fourth Circuit refused to grant a preliminary injunction. A group of students at UNC continued this case, claiming that the program violated their rights under the Free Exercise Clause of the First Amendment. The district court soundly rejected the students' claim for several key reasons: first, UNC had a clearly established policy that allowed any student to refrain from reading the book, and the district court also noted that the book was not a religious reading but rather should be characterized as an academic reading. In granting summary judgment for the defendants in the case, the district court concluded: "UNC implemented a program asking students to discuss a religion thrust into recent controversy, and to do so from an academic perspective. Part of the purpose of this program was to introduce students to the type of higher-level thinking that is required in a university setting. Students who were not members of the Islamic faith, probably the great majority of students, were neither asked nor forced to give up their own beliefs or to compromise their own beliefs in order to discuss the patterns, language, history, and cultural significance of the Qur'an" (324 F.Supp.2d 764).

Taken together, these cases demonstrate that religion and spirituality is clearly an acceptable topic of discussion in public higher education (*Yacovelli* v. *Moeser,* 2004), but institutions must also take into consideration students' rights when compelling speech (*Axson-Flynn* v. *Johnson,* 2004).

In considering the issue of faculty speech in the classroom, issues of academic freedom also come into play. The leading case regarding this intersection of religion and academic freedom is *Bishop* v. *Aronov* (1991). Bishop taught courses in exercise physiology and would occasionally mention his religious beliefs in the classroom, a practice about which some students complained. Bishop was ordered by the university to discontinue this practice, at which time he brought suit against the university, claiming that this action was a violation of his academic freedom. The Court of Appeals for the Eleventh Circuit ruled for the institution, citing "the university's authority in matters of course content as superior to that of the professor" (Kaplin and Lee, 1995, p. 310). However, several commentators have suggested that the court may not have been sensitive enough to Bishop's academic freedom claims (Kaplin and Lee, 1995; O'Neil, 1997).

More recently, James Tuttle, an adjunct professor of philosophy at Lakeland Community College (Mentor, Ohio), sued the institution, claiming that he was being punished for discussing his religious beliefs in the classroom (Evelyn, 2004). Although this case has not been tried, it clearly indicates that these issues are far from resolved. Furthermore, the courses that Tuttle taught, philosophy and religion, have direct bearing on his claim.

O'Neil (1997) noted that the relevancy of the professor's religious beliefs to the course subject must be considered when determining the effects of academic freedom on the matter.

Spirituality Outside the Classroom

Institutions of higher education must also carefully consider the legal implications of addressing issues related to spirituality and religion outside of the classroom, especially student-initiated religious expression. The area in which these issues most often arise is related to the relationship between the institution and student religious groups. Often this confusion stems from an overemphasis of the Establishment Clause of the First Amendment without fully considering the Free Speech and Free Exercise clauses. Summarizing the rights of college students, Kaplin and Lee (1995) concluded that students have a "general right to organize; to be officially recognized whenever the school has a policy of recognizing student groups; and to use meeting rooms, bulletin boards, and similar facilities open to student groups" (p. 516).

In *Healy* v. *James* (1972), the Supreme Court ruled that Central Connecticut State College had violated the students' association rights under the First Amendment when the president refused to recognize as a student organization a local chapter of the Students for a Democratic Society (SDS). The court concluded that this decision was based largely on the president's disagreement with SDS's philosophy. In describing association rights, the court observed, "While the freedom of association is not explicitly set out in the [First] Amendment, it has long been held to be implicit in the freedom of speech, assembly, and petition. There can be no doubt that denial of official recognition, without justification, to college organizations burdens or abridges that associational right" (408 U.S. 181). The court acknowledged that this was not absolute, however. There are three specific situations in which a public college or university would be justified in its refusal to recognize a student organization:

- The group has a known "affiliation with an organization possessing unlawful aims and goals, and a specific intent to further those illegal goals" (408 U.S. 186).
- The group poses a "substantial threat of material disruption through its conduct" (408 U.S. 189).
- The group refuses to comply with "reasonable school rules governing conduct" (408 U.S. 191).

The courts specifically addressed the issues involving student religious organizations in *Aman* v. *Handler* (1981). In this case, the University of New Hampshire refused to recognize a campus chapter of the Collegiate Association for Research of Principles (CARP), an organization that allegedly had ties with Reverend Sun Myung Moon and the Unification Church. Although the institution attempted to justify its decision through an exemption articulated in *Healy,* the court ruled for the students and ruled that the group be recognized.

Beyond the recognition of student religious organizations, institutions must also consider issues related to access, space, and funding for student organizations. In *Widmar* v. *Vincent* (1981), the Supreme Court ruled that once a public institution allows student groups access to university facilities, a student religious organization could not be denied access to the same facilities for religious services. Justice Powell observed, "Having created a forum generally open to student groups, the University seeks to enforce a content-based exclusion of religious speech. Its exclusionary policy violates the fundamental principle that a state regulation of speech should be content-neutral" (454 U.S. 277). Kaplin and Lee (1997) warned that this ruling did not allow institutions to create facilities specifically for religious groups.

The Supreme Court expanded its *Widmar* (1981) decision to apply to the distribution of mandatory student-activity fees in *Rosenberger* v. *Rector and Visitors of University of Virginia* (1995). The Supreme Court ruled that the University of Virginia had created a "metaphysical" forum by funding student organizations (515 U.S. 830). Once the university began to pay for the printing of student publications, the institution could not refuse to pay for the printing of *Wide Awake,* a student Christian publication, because of the religious viewpoint it expressed. Justice Kennedy wrote in his opinion, "The University does not exclude religion as a subject matter but selects for disfavored treatment those student journalistic efforts with religious editorial viewpoints" (515 U.S. 831). The Supreme Court returned to the question of the constitutionality of mandatory student activity fees in *Board of Regents of University of Wisconsin System* v. *Southworth* (2000). Justice Kennedy concluded, "The First Amendment permits a public university to charge its students an activity fee used to fund a program to facilitate extracurricular student speech if the program [by which funds are allocated] is viewpoint neutral" (529 U.S. 251).

Conclusion

With the resurgent interest in both spirituality in higher education and traditional religious expression in American society and on campus, it is absolutely vital that faculty and administrators are familiar with legal implications. As this chapter has noted, legal questions do not often lend themselves to simple answers. Institutions must be mindful of two seemingly conflicting obligations: to respect students' right to the free exercise of their religious beliefs and to avoid violating the Establishment Clause by unconstitutionally favoring religion.

References

Aman v. Handler, 653 F.2d 41 (1st Cir. 1981).
Axson-Flynn v. Johnson, 356 F.3d 1277 (10th Cir. 2004).
Bishop v. Aronov, 926 F.2d 1066 (11th Cir. 1991).

Board of Regents of University of Wisconsin System v. Southworth, 529 U.S. 217 (2000).
Brown, S. P. *Trumping Religion: The New Christian Right, the Free Speech Clause, and the Courts.* Tuscaloosa, Ala.: University of Alabama Press, 2002.
Chaudhuri v. Tennessee, 130 F.3d 232 (6th Cir. 1997), cert. denied, 523 U.S. 1024 (1998).
Clark, R. T. "The Law and Spirituality: How the Law Supports and Limits Expression of Spirituality on the College Campus." In M. A. Jablonski (ed.), The Implications of Student Spirituality for Student Affairs Practice. New Directions for Student Services, no. 95. San Francisco: Jossey-Bass, 2001.
Employment Division, Department of Human Resources of Oregon v. Smith, 494 U.S. 872 (1990).
Engel v. Vitale, 370 U.S. 421 (1962).
Evelyn, J. "Saying He Was Punished for Revealing His Faith, Adjunct Sues Ohio College." *Chronicle of Higher Education,* Jul. 16, 2004, p. A13.
Healy v. James, 408 U.S. 169 (1972).
Kaplin, W. A., and Lee, B. A. *The Law of Higher Education.* (3rd ed.) San Francisco: Jossey-Bass, 1995.
Kaplin, W. A., and Lee, B. A. *A Legal Guide for Student Affairs Professionals.* San Francisco: Jossey-Bass, 1997.
Klein, A. "Supreme Court Declines to Hear Virginia Military Institute's Prayer Case." *Chronicle of Higher Education,* May 7, 2004, p. A40.
Lee v. Weisman, 505 U.S. 577 (1992).
Lemon v. Kurtzman, 403 U.S. 602 (1971).
Locke v. Davey, 540 U.S. 712 (2004).
Lowery, J. W. "*Walking the Halls of Ivy with Christ: The Classroom and Residential Experiences of Undergraduate Evangelical Students.*" Unpublished doctoral dissertation, Bowling Green State University, Bowling Green, Ohio, 2000.
Lowery, J. W. "Understanding the Legal Protections and Limitations upon Religion and Spiritual Expression on Campus." *College Student Affairs Journal,* 2004, 23, 146–157.
Mellen v. Bunting, 327 F.3d 355 (4th Cir. 2003), cert. denied, 541 U.S. 1019 (2004).
O'Neil, R. M. *Free Speech in the College Community.* Bloomington: Indiana University Press, 1997.
Rosenberger v. Rector and Visitors of University of Virginia, 515 U.S. 819 (1995).
Santa Fe Independent School District v. Doe, 530 U.S. 290 (2000).
School District of Abington Township v. Schempp, 374 U.S. 203 (1963).
Sells, M. A. *Approaching the Qur'an: The Early Revelations.* Ashland, Ore.: White Cloud Press, 1999.
Settle v. Dickson County School Board, 53 F.3d 152 (6th Cir. 1995).
Sherbert v. Verner, 374 U.S. 398 (1963).
Tanford v. Brand, 104 F.3d 982 (7th Cir. 1997), cert. denied, 522 U.S. 814 (1997).
Tilton v. Richardson, 403 U.S. 672 (1971).
Wallace v. Jaffree, 472 U.S. 38 (1985).
West Virginia Board of Education v. Barnette, 319 U.S. 624 (1943).
Widmar v. Vincent, 454 U.S. 263 (1981).
Wisconsin v. Yoder, 406 U.S. 205 (1972).
Yacovelli v. Moeser, 324 F.Supp.2d 760 (M.D.N.C. 2004).

JOHN WESLEY LOWERY is assistant professor of higher education and student affairs in the Department of Educational Leadership and Policies at the University of South Carolina at Columbia where he teaches courses in student affairs in higher education, legal issues in higher education, and student development theory.

3

The spiritual identity of the academy is historically based, and changes in that identity pose special problems for the search for truth in contemporary times.

The Academy, Spirituality, and the Search for Truth

Christina Murphy

In *American Higher Education: A History,* Lucas (1994) states that the American university has evolved through three stages of emphasis and growth. In the earliest phase, from the founding of Harvard University in 1636 to the era before the Civil War, the purpose of the American university was to educate the individual to higher knowledge and to a sense of purpose that included an awareness of the soul's relationship to God. The founders of the American universities and colleges in this era were largely members of the clergy, and the relationship of the academic institution to the community was that of a civic trust in which the community and the institution shared a common sense of purpose that ensued as civic engagement for the common good or common wealth of the whole.

By the end of the nineteenth century, the role of the American university as an extension and enactment of the religious and spiritual values of the community had changed to the view of the academy as a research institution dedicated to the exploration of knowledge as a means of investigating and mastering science and technology—often at the expense of and in contrast to spiritual explorations and understandings of the natural world. Scientific progress dominated the imagination of this era as the promises of the Industrial Revolution and the continuing rise of science and technology reconfigured the sense of purpose for the academy. Aronowitz and Giroux (1985) in *Education Under Siege* indicate that this period marked the rise of the conservative perspective in which education is regarded as a type of regimented and highly authoritarian training for future work roles within society.

NEW DIRECTIONS FOR TEACHING AND LEARNING, no. 104, Winter 2005   © Wiley Periodicals, Inc.

The third stage began roughly after World War II, bringing the domination of a business model for education. Issues like "total quality management" and the bottom line began to replace concerns for academic integrity and community service as the central goals of higher education. Certainly, this phase has also witnessed the ascendance of the for-profit universities as a major component of higher education and often as the exemplar of how contemporary education should be productive, cost-effective, and streamlined to meet the needs and demands of a global workforce.

Philosophical Outcomes of the Three Stages

The outcome of these three stages is a shift in higher education's focus from community ideals of shared values that also encompass a sense of the intellectual, moral, and spiritual dimensions in education, to the view of higher education as a business or corporation that functions to sustain capitalism and to supply the workforce. Certainly, the reduction in state funding for higher education, in concert with the ability of for-profit institutions to donate to political campaigns and sway legislation in their favor (Burd, 2004), has intensified the transformation of the American university as a social institution. In many ways, the American university is now often indistinguishable from a corporation—with trademarked logos, advertising deals, income from sponsored ventures (especially athletics), and incentive packages for the hiring of university presidents—and so the influence of the university on society has also changed dramatically.

The greatest impact has been on the role of character education, which in earlier times was the most important role that education carried out in society. Character education has gone by many names over the years but has been united by a sense of educating students to moral values and for a moral purpose within the world. Certainly, the decline in a focus on community values has also meant that the significant role education played in conveying the moral values of society from one generation to the next has been modified—if not nullified—by this substantial alteration of higher education.

Holistic View Versus Science and Technology

The emphasis on character education represents an attempt to return to a lost ideal of spirituality in education—an ideal based on a holistic understanding of the individual student as a person seeking truth and understanding. Within the matrices of inquiry that the student could pursue, spirituality was accepted as a way of knowing and as a means of interpretation and thus understanding and meaning. The rise of the American research university as a twentieth-century response to a growing belief in and dependence on science and technology replaced the holistic view of truth and of education with a unified sense of education as a scientific search for one truth—or "the truth"—about the nature of reality. The idea of multiple interpretations fell out of favor or came to be regarded as the preoccupation of liberal arts colleges and not the philosophical realm of a "true" (that is, research) university.

This emphasis was intensified by famed scientist Vannevar Bush's 1945 government report titled *Science: The Endless Frontier* in which Bush argued for major federal funding initiatives toward higher education in support of large-scale scientific research. Bush presented a new model of federal involvement in "big science"—or the process of competitive grants submitted by university research scientists to carry out government-funded projects. Such initiatives, in essence, argued for and represented federal policies toward higher education, as distinguished from public policies. They also redefined the purpose of the university as a research complex funded in large measure by government and industry. The goal of educating students and preparing them for a life of service and civic engagement became, at best, a secondary emphasis.

Thus, it is no wonder that Buckley's 1951 book, *God and Man at Yale: The Superstitions of Academic Freedom,* won such a responsive national audience when Buckley argued that his alma mater, Yale University, had lost its way in no longer educating socially responsive individuals. Instead, this once-conservative university with its traditional commitment to political order and to religious beliefs had now surrendered itself to moral relativism and to a measure of ivory-tower thinking that removed the institution from focusing on social issues. Veysey (1970) took this concept further by arguing that the loss of a unified vision for the purpose of education led to the establishment of large bureaucracies within universities. These bureaucracies in turn fostered a culture of synthesis and compromise from which emerged a standard American university that functioned relatively effectively but that pleased no single group philosophically in its commitments and goals.

In many ways, Buckley (1951) and Veysey (1970) are criticizing the American university and the process of higher education for not being grounded in traditional principles and thus losing their identity to the commercialism and popular trends of an aimless society. This concept is one that Kerr (1963) explores in *The Uses of the University,* and certainly such a perspective also supports the postmodern ideas of the loss of moral values in the contemporary world—ideas that have been explored by many philosophers, most notably Cutler (1997) in *Rediscovering Values: Coming to Terms with Postmodernism.*

Nature of Liberal Arts Education

A number of educational theorists trace this eclipse of moral values within higher education to the decline of a liberal arts education and of the traditions associated with the liberal arts (Farnham and Yarmolinsky, 1996;

Gless and Smith, 1992; Kerr, 1963; Mitias, 1992; Nussbaum, 1997; Young, 1999). One basis for this concern is that the liberal arts have traditionally been associated with disciplines that invite students to explore the meaning of their humanity and to consider what it means to be a citizen of the world, with all the concomitant moral issues, challenges, and calls to action involved with such an analysis. Thus, the changing landscape of education has devalued, if not marginalized, the liberal arts because of education's increasing emphasis on disciplines that translate easily and well to workplace skills and high employment rates. The liberal arts, with their emphasis on core studies that provide foundation-building skills for critical thinking, analytical skills, communication and interpersonal skills, and a broad awareness of cultural traditions, generally do not fit the employment emphasis that higher education must pursue in a competitive environment in which the number of students who graduate and find jobs is often used as one marker of success for the institution in meeting its goals and its commitments to the community and the nation.

Adding more complexity to this issue is that the liberal arts themselves derive from ancient and medieval theories that provide a different sense of what it means to be human in the world. The *artes liberales* were conceived as the studies or explorations of disciplines that served to "free" the person, in contrast to the *artes illiberales* that are pursued for economic purposes. This contrast in the purpose of education is stark, indeed, but perhaps not so striking as the contrast in the definitions and understandings of truth. Is the purpose of education to prepare students to seek the truths of their individuality and of their purpose in the world, or is the purpose of education to prepare students for the workforce and employment opportunities they will encounter on the completion of their education? In earlier times, two ideals predominated in higher education: the concern for the fullest development of the individual student's potential (*cura personalis*) and the belief that the university acted in loco parentis in assuming the duties and responsibilities of the parent in continuing to shape the intellectual and spiritual formation of the student. To see how far we have moved from this second ideal, the 2002 edition of *The New Dictionary of Cultural Literacy* states in its definition of *in loco parentis* that "at one time, colleges and universities acted *in loco parentis* for their students, but this is no longer true" (Hirsch, Kett, and Trefil, p. 70).

This difference in outlook and in the truth value of an education is especially important when related to the ideals of education associated with the Middle Ages and especially with its most important scholastic philosopher, St. Thomas Aquinas. In the *Summa Theologica* (1273), Aquinas identified the pursuit of knowledge with love and thus with the deepest aspects of the person's individual soul or spirit. In essence, Aquinas argued that what a person loves, he seeks to know; and what a person seeks to know, he loves. Thus, each person will pursue knowledge (and thus a course of action) on the basis of love, or more precisely, on the basis of the relationship of the intellect to love. Love is the moral foundation of the pursuit of knowledge because the intellect seeks after truth, and to Aquinas and the Middle Ages, the highest source of truth is God, or the divine.

This concept of the individual informs the *artes liberales* as well in that there is no distinction between educating the person to pursue knowledge and educating the person to act as an expression of that love. Associated with a deep love and longing for knowledge are such virtues as commitment, dedication, selflessness, and desire, for how else to explain the lonely passions and dedications of those who pursue greater knowledge in a given field or area due to their great love for the knowledge they pursue?

Education and the Search for Truth

Thus, it is a larger issue to be concerned about the decline of the liberal arts in contemporary times than merely a sense that the liberal arts have served their time in having greater relevance to a nonindustrial world than to a highly technological, postmodern one. It is truly a debate not only about what is the purpose of education, but as well about what is the highest purpose for a human life and what spiritual truths that individual will pursue and why.

Those who would wish to restore the traditional sense of the liberal arts are often charged with holding reactionary views that seek to negate contemporary realities. However, the struggle to define moral values continues and often redefines itself in more acceptable terms like "civic engagement" or "service learning" in which students can still experience the sense of identifying knowledge with moral purposes and pursuits. Cardoza and Salinas (2004), for example, argue in "Public Citizen: The Civic Role of an Educational Institution for the Betterment of Society" that higher education institutions should exemplify and thus be engaged in creating within students an "impetus toward civic duty" (p. 30).

Liberal and Conservative Traditions

Certainly, the issues that Cardoza and Salinas (2004) and many others raise with regard to the purpose of higher education place the debate clearly within the two competing traditions that Aronowitz and Giroux (1985) identify as the liberal and the conservative, or that ancient and medieval traditions identify as the *artes liberales* and the *artes illiberales*. Whether higher education in the contemporary world should exist to meet workforce and employment needs and thus to function as a corporation in pursuing economic ends is a central question of our era, as Slaughter and Leslie (1999) discuss in their aptly titled book *Academic Capitalism: Politics, Policies, and the Entrepreneurial*.

No doubt the emergence of the entrepreneurial university as a business entity that must generate most (if not all) of its funding and must compete with for-profit institutions to deliver the most efficient means of workforce preparation is a challenge to conventional definitions of higher education. It is a challenge, too, to traditional understandings of the student as an individual with particular talents and abilities that are nurtured, enhanced, and empowered through the educational process. The loss of this perspective is troubling to many educational theorists who see in this conceptual framework a spiritual understanding of the individual and his or her search for truth. To these theorists, the search for economic success is not the highest ideal to which higher education should be committed. Instead, some offer— like O'Brien (2000) in *All the Essential Half-Truths About Higher Education*— dramatic, if not radical, calls for a return to a different modality for carrying out the role of higher education as a public trust and a civic good. O'Brien, for example, calls for a return to the earliest historical ideal of American higher education in which small, denominational colleges predominated and determined the purposes of education. At the center of such colleges was the president as a powerful leader with a moral vision that unified the faculty and the institution with an imbued sense of moral purpose.

Although it is unlikely that American higher education will devolve the extensive, expensive, and highly entrenched research universities and transform them into a series of small, denominational colleges, at the very least we can agree with Brubacher and Rudy (1997) that American higher education is "in transition" from these earlier ideals toward an uncertain identity. The central issue on which that transition will rest is that of purpose and whether purpose itself will be separated from the long-held belief that education is a civic good because it prepares students for citizenship and equips them with a moral sense of responsibility to the world. Shall that view of purpose prevail, or will it be the view that the American university exists to sponsor research, educate the next generation of workers, and pursue economic and entrepreneurial ideals in support of capitalism?

Conclusion

Certainly, Lucas (1994) is perceptive in arguing that throughout the history of American education, knowledge has been a "social construction" between the institution and the society it serves. So we can anticipate that the terms of this engagement will evolve and differ as the society itself grapples with the issues of what constitutes knowledge, truth, education, and even the individual intellect and spirit. No doubt, different views of each aspect will grapple for ascendancy, and thus the debate over the nature of truth and of spirituality will continue as long as this central dynamic of the role of higher education continues to play itself out as a struggle between half-truths (O'Brien, 2000), liberal and conservative values (Aronowitz and Giroux, 1985), or the medieval view of the individual as a seeker after spiritual truths that intersect in the relationship of mind, spirit, and ultimate reality.

References

Aronowitz, S., and Giroux, H. A. *Education Under Siege*. South Hadley, Mass.: Bergin & Garvey, 1985.

Aquinas, St. Thomas. *Summa Theologica*. (Fathers of the English Dominican Province, trans.). Notre Dame, Ind.: Ave Maria Press, 1981.

Brubacher, J. S., and Rudy, W. *Higher Education in Transition: A History of American Colleges and Universities*. Somerset, N.J.: Transaction Publishers, 1997.

Buckley, W. F. *God and Man at Yale: The Superstitions of Academic Freedom. Reprint of the 1951 Edition with a New Introduction by the Author*. Washington, D.C.: Regnery Gateway, 1978.

Burd, S. "For-Profit Colleges Spend Big and Win Big on Capitol Hill." *Chronicle of Higher Education*, Jul. 30, 2004, p. A19.

Bush, V. *Science: The Endless Frontier; A Report to the President by Vannevar Bush, Director of the Office of Scientific Research and Development, July 1945*. Washington, D.C.: Government Printing Office, 1945.

Cardoza, O., and Salinas, G. "Public Citizen: The Civic Role of an Educational Institution for the Betterment of Society." In K. Ferraiolo (ed.), *New Directions in Civic Engagement: University Avenue Meets Main Street*. Richmond, Va.: Pew Partnership for Civic Change/University of Richmond, 2004.

Cutler, H. M. *Rediscovering Values: Coming to Terms with Postmodernism*. Armonk, N.Y.: Sharpe, 1997.

Farnham, N. H., and Yarmolinsky, A. *Rethinking Liberal Education*. New York: Oxford University Press, 1996.

Gless, D. J., and Smith, B. H. (eds.). *The Politics of Liberal Education*. Durham, N.C.: Duke University Press, 1992.

Hirsch, E. D., Jr., Kett, J. F., and Trefil, J. (eds.). *The New Dictionary of Cultural Literacy*. New York: Houghton Mifflin, 2002.

Kerr, C. *The Uses of the University*. Cambridge, Mass.: Harvard University Press, 1963.

Lucas, C. J. *American Higher Education: A History*. New York: St. Martin's Griffin, 1994.

Mitias, M. H. (ed.). *Moral Education and the Liberal Arts*. Westport, Conn.: Greenwood Press, 1992.

Nussbaum, M. C. *Cultivating Humanity: A Classical Defense of Reform in Liberal Education*. Cambridge, Mass.: Harvard University Press, 1997.

O'Brien, G. D. *All the Essential Half-Truths about Higher Education*. Chicago: University of Chicago Press, 2000.

Slaughter, S., and Leslie, L. L. *Academic Capitalism: Politics, Policies, and the Entrepreneurial*. Baltimore: Johns Hopkins University Press, 1999.

Veysey, L. *The Emergence of the American University*. Chicago: University of Chicago Press, 1970.

Young, R. V. *At War with the Word: Literary Theory and Liberal Education*. Wilmington, Del.: ISI Books, 1999.

CHRISTINA MURPHY *is dean of the College of Liberal Arts and professor of English at Marshall University in Huntington, West Virginia.*

4

Educating the whole student requires addressing spiritual development and is best accomplished through an integration of academic and student affairs.

Role of Spirituality and Spiritual Development in Student Life Outside the Classroom

Jennifer Capeheart-Meningall

College is a critical time when students search for meaning in life and examine their spiritual beliefs and values. During this time, students are asking questions about meaning and morality, belief and behavior (Garber, 1996). How do students learn to conscientiously connect what they believe and how they live? According to Garber, "The years between adolescence and adulthood are crucial, moral meaning is being formed and central to the formation is a vision of integrity which coherently connects belief to behavior personally as well as publicly" (p. 20). Indeed, "true education is always about learning to connect knowing with doing, belief with behavior . . . " (p. 43). The challenge for colleges and universities is thus to educate students holistically. This requires providing programs and activities that emphasize social, physical, intellectual, career, psychological, cultural, and spiritual development. One of the most sensitive and potentially controversial—and the subject of this chapter—is spiritual development.

Spiritual development is an integral part of overall student development and learning. The role of student affairs in spiritual development is critical because of the commitment to provide purposeful programs that address the integrated whole of students' development and learning.

Spirituality and Spiritual Development

According to Tisdell (2003), "Spirituality is one of the ways people construct knowledge and meaning" (p. 20). Tisdell is not discussing religion, defined as a shared system of beliefs, principles, and doctrine related to an organized community of faith. Instead, spirituality defines how people construct knowledge through meaning-making and awareness of wholeness and the interconnectedness of all things, including unconscious and symbolic processes (Tisdell, 2003).

Discussions of spirituality in the academy often involve transformative learning. This learning considers "what students know, who they are, what their values and behavior patterns are, and how they see themselves contributing to and participating in the world in which they live" (Keeling, 2004, p. 10). By this, we encourage intentional, engaged, and empowered learners who integrate knowledge, skills, and experiences to make meaning throughout their lives. Consequently, spirituality can direct daily living that consistently exemplifies self-integration, which is holistic, involving physical, psychological, and social aspects of the individual, bringing all aspects of life together in relation to others in his or her world.

Jablonski (2001) said, "Spiritual development is a form of deeper learning because it touches on students' encounter with transcendence and ultimate meaning in their lives" (p. 19). Spiritual development, an ongoing and continuous process, is about students' personal quests for clarifying and fulfilling personal destiny. Although difficult to measure, spiritual development provides opportunities to have deeper and sustainable learning experiences in college.

Love and Talbot (1999) utilize five interrelated processes to define spiritual development: "Spiritual development involves (1) an internal process of seeking personal authenticity, genuineness, and wholeness as an aspect of identity development, . . . (2) the process of continually transcending one's current locus of centricity, . . . (3) developing a greater connectedness to self and others through relationships and union with community, . . . (4) deriving meaning, purpose, and direction in one's life, and . . . (5) increasing openness to exploring a relationship with an intangible and pervasive power or essence that exists beyond human existence and rational human knowing" (pp. 364–367).

Love and Talbot's (1999) process of spiritual development consistently supports student development theory that advocates integrating all aspects of students' learning. Students' histories, social interactions, families, religion, values, and so forth provide the framework to make meaning of newly acquired information. "Adults, some of whom are students, constantly acquire information, examine its implications, apply it to areas of understanding and action that are personally significant, and reframe their insights as circumstances evolved through a process of transformative learning" (Keeling, 2004, p. 11). Tisdell (2003) notes that integrating life experiences and developing a critical reflective process of self, coupled with the academic learning environment, will facilitate knowledge construction in both students and educators. Love and Talbot's (1999) process of spiritual development becomes the bridge between the life currently being lived and the life students are developing through the integration of new knowledge with old.

Student and Academic Affairs Collaboration in Spiritual Development

Students are in a continual process of growth and change, regardless of college attendance; however, the question is what influence the college experience has on that change. The collaboration of student and academic affairs can have a positive influence by providing a seamless opportunity to "promote, challenge, validate, and build on new and previous learning" (Maki, 2003, p. 2). This type of learning, which is considered transformative, based on intentional partnering, can shape students' learning and development in productive ways.

Spiritual development is critical both to the integrated development of the student and to the fulfillment of our responsibility to educate the whole student. Attending to spiritual development through student and academic affairs' programs and services will vary based on the collegiate setting, organization, and priorities. Notwithstanding, focusing on spirituality and spiritual development can result in learning outcomes that lead to personal and social transformation in students. The National Study of College Students' Search for Meaning and Purpose–Summary of Findings (Astin and others, 2004) noted the following initial outcomes to be positively associated with spirituality:

- Physical and psychological health, including self-esteem
- Optimism and a sense of personal empowerment
- Civic responsibility, including charitable involvement and social activism
- Empathy, understanding and caring for others, including the importance of reducing pain and suffering in the world, feeling a strong connection to all humanity, compassionate self-concept
- Racial or ethnic awareness and tolerance, including the importance of promoting racial understanding, attending racial or cultural awareness workshops, the ability to get along with people of different race or cultures, and growth in tolerance during college
- Academic performance, including graduate-level degree aspiration and intellectual self-confidence
- Satisfaction with college, including a sense of community on campus, the amount of contact with faculty, interaction with other students, and overall college experience
- Religiousness, including religious commitment and involvement [pp. 10–12]

This preliminary list solidifies the importance of including spiritual development in the work of student affairs. These outcomes not only aid students in their quest to obtain a degree but also provide a deeper learning experience. Thus, student and academic affairs must work to transcend boundaries that hinder the creation of out-of-classroom programs and activities that enhance students' undergraduate experience. Incorporating spiritual development will require new ways of thinking, a review of campus learning environments, an analysis of patterns and methods of program delivery and systems, and possibly a divisional realignment to honor educating the integrated whole of the student.

Infusing Spiritual Development in Student Life Outside the Classroom

Approaches to operationalizing spiritual development into student and academic affairs programs and services include the following:

• *One, spiritual development involves an internal process of seeking personal authenticity, genuineness, and wholeness as an aspect of identity development.* This developmental aspect can be achieved by incorporating student values clarification and goal setting into initial orientation programs. Learning communities, counseling sessions, judicial processes, leadership programs, and first-year career development activities can also engage students to identify the values and principles that govern their behaviors. "All campus educators should ensure the establishment of reflection and other meaning-making opportunities for students to examine the breadth of their learning (e.g., through portfolios, advising, journals, life planning, mentoring programs)" (Keeling, 2004, p. 29). Assisting students to live and behave in congruence with their own principles will strengthen the connection between what they believe and how they behave. Chavez (2001) states that "living reflectively is perhaps the most foundational of all the principles I live by; it affects my ability to live by all of the others [principles]" (p. 73). As educators, we must work to design our campus environments where reflective analysis is prevalent. This type of reflection allows students to make meaning out of what they are learning, what they believe, and what they are doing.

• *Two, spiritual development involves the process of continually transcending one's current locus of centricity.* Learning to live a balanced life is critical in assisting students to develop spiritually. Chavez (2001) indicates, "Balance involves living in balance with all life forms, and living in healthy ways every day" (p. 74). Programs and activities that teach students life-management skills in all aspects will assist them in achieving balance (for example, wellness programs, time and stress management, building healthy relationships).

• *Three, spiritual development involves developing a greater connectedness to self and others through relationships and union with community.*

"Shared purpose, shared commitment, shared relationships, shared responsibility—the need for community is a primal yearning and a practical necessity in our lives and in our society" (McDonald, 2002, p. 3). Programs and services that offer activities that affirm diversity, establish and hold students accountable for conduct, celebrate campus traditions, and join various constituencies together will help build community. Volunteerism and community service programs are other activities that correlate strongly with building a unified vision of the campus and surrounding community.

• *Four, spiritual development involves deriving meaning, purpose, and direction in one's life.* Programs and services that allow students to explore interests and skills, personal goal setting and calling, and self-exploration and -understanding will encourage students to fulfill their life's purpose. Activities such as support groups, residential dialogues, campus ministries, career explorations, and life planning allow students to solidify their search for their own purpose.

• *Five, spiritual development involves increasing openness to exploring a relationship with an intangible and pervasive power or essence that exists beyond human existence and rational human being.* Any program that addresses spirituality and spiritual development has the potential to strengthen students' educational gains. Specifically, campus ministries, religious student organizations, and lectures on various religions are examples of activities that support this developmental element.

Conclusion

It is incumbent on student and academic affairs administrators to acknowledge the impact of out-of-classroom experience on educational gains. Students involved in out-of-classroom programs are more positive about their overall collegiate experience, more satisfied with their social lives, have more contact with faculty, and are more likely to graduate than other students (Kuh, Schuh, Whitt, and Associates, 1991). Because students spend most of their time out of class, it is crucial for institutions to deliberately design programs for transformative learning. Including spiritual development enhances the educational experience of the student and promotes holistic learning. To the extent that educating the whole student is possible, incorporating spiritual development underscores the potential to facilitate transformative learning.

References

Astin, A., and others. "Spirituality in Higher Education: A National Study of College Students Search for Meaning and Purpose." Higher Education Research Institute, University of California, Los Angeles, 2004. http://www.spirituality.ucla.edu. Accessed Apr. 28, 2004.

Chavez, A. F. "Spirit and Nature in Everyday Life: Reflections of a *Mestiza* in Higher Education." In M. A. Jablonski (ed.), *The Implications of Student Spirituality for Student*

Affairs Practice. New Directions for Student Services, no. 95. San Francisco: Jossey-Bass, 2001.

Garber, S. *The Fabric of Faithfulness: Weaving Together Belief and Behavior During the University Years.* Downers Grove, Ill.: InterVarsity Press, 1996.

Jablonski, M. A. (ed.). *The Implications of Student Spirituality for Student Affairs Practice.* New Directions for Student Services, no. 95. San Francisco: Jossey-Bass, 2001.

Keeling, P. R. (ed.). *Learning Reconsidered: A Campus-Wide Focus on the Student Experience.* Washington, D.C.: American College Personnel Association and National Association of Student Personnel Administrators, 2004.

Kuh, G. D., Schuh, J. H., Whitt, E. J., and Associates. *Involving Colleges: Successful Approaches to Fostering Student Learning and Development Outside the Classroom.* San Francisco: Jossey-Bass, 1991.

Love, P., and Talbot, D. "Defining Spiritual Development: A Missing Consideration for Student Affairs." *NASPA Journal,* 1999, 37(1), 361–375.

Maki, P. *Learning Contexts Inside and Outside of the Academy.* Washington, D.C.: American Association of Higher Education, 2003.

McDonald, W. (ed.). *Creating Campus Community: In Search of Ernest Boyer's Legacy.* San Francisco: Jossey-Bass, 2002.

Tisdell, E. *Exploring Spirituality and Culture in Adult and Higher Education.* San Francisco: Jossey-Bass, 2003.

JENNIFER CAPEHEART-MENINGALL *is vice president for student affairs at the University of South Florida in Tampa.*

5

*Spirituality may have a genetic base, but the resulting
predisposition does not direct specific beliefs.*

Spirituality: The Physiological-Biological Foundation

Thomas J. Buttery, Philip S. Roberson

The spiritual dimension evokes feelings of faith, love, hope, awe, trust, and inspiration and provides a meaning and a reason for existence. A spiritual person, according to Campbell (2003), is continuously devoted to creating, honoring, and acting out those aspects of the self that are reflective of higher values. Moreover, the spiritual person is concerned with a sense of purpose and meaning in life and seeks to share this with others.

Whereas Burkhardt (1989) describes spirituality as harmonious inter-connectedness, with mystic unfolding, Narayanasamy (1999) postulates that it is rooted in an awareness that is part of the physiological-biological makeup of human beings. Spirituality manifests itself as inner peace and strength derived from a perceived relationship with a deity.

Spirituality and religion are overlapping but separate concepts (Pargament and others, 1995; Zinnbauer and others, 1997). Religion is a cultural process and presents ways of behaving and relating that are intended to facilitate people living together in relative harmony and pro-ductivity. Spirituality is based in consciousness; it is universal and is believed to have a genetic predisposition.

Consciousness

Albright and Ashbrook (2001) and Hamer (2004) concur that the way we perceive the world relates directly to spirituality. The mediating force of spirituality is consciousness: the awareness and understanding of our sur-roundings. Chalmers (1997) indicates that ". . . conscious experience is at once the most familiar thing in the world and the most mysterious" (p. 1).

Theories about consciousness abound (for example, try a simple Google search).

Simplistically put, core consciousness is how the brain processes basic stimuli of the senses. Higher consciousness relates to individuals' perceptions of the world around them. Through higher consciousness, humans can manipulate abstract concepts and perceive themselves in relation to those abstractions. Spirituality functions in the sphere of higher consciousness.

Philosophically, a mind-body debate has been going on since the time of Aristotle and Plato. Aristotle contended that the mind and body were two parts of the same whole; however, Plato believed that the soul was distinct from the body and could survive outside it. Today "materialists" believe that consciousness can be expressed in terms of principles of chemistry and physics. However, "dualists" hold to an explanation of consciousness that invokes principles above natural law.

Edelman (1992), a Nobel Prize winner in biology, has developed a scientific theory of consciousness. His paradigm indicates that the brain's thalamocortical system generates perceptual categories. The brain matches these categories with value messages that originate in the limbic or brain-stem system. This values-category system is cycled back through the thalamo-cortical system for additional categorization, creating a loop of correlations between events and categories. Hamer (2004) maintains that what is unique about human consciousness is the ability to associate scenes and senses with emotions and values.

Examining Spirituality

During the past two decades, the study of neuroscience has made tremendous strides in bridging the gap between the human and physical sciences. The sophisticated tools of neuroscience allow us to study inner experience through empirical investigation. A basic tenet of human behavior is that we are meaning-seeking creatures. The scientific explanations that are being discovered relate more to why and how humans believe, not whether those beliefs are valid or true.

Consistent with scientific study, the question has to be asked, "Is spirituality a measurable trait?" According to Cloninger (1994), the developer of the Temperament and Character Inventory (TCI), it is. One of the subtests of the TCI measures self-transcendence, a term used to describe feelings of spirituality that are independent of traditional religious percepts. For example, self-transcendence is autonomous of belief in a specific God and is independent of the frequency of prayer, church-religious attendance, and other orthodox manifestations of religious practice.

The attribute of self-transcendence can be disaggregated into three traits:

• Self-forgetfulness, or the capacity to be completely absorbed in an experience; for instance, hours can pass in what seem to be moments

- Transpersonal identification, which relates to the feeling of connectedness to a larger universe, characterized by strong emotional attachment to people, animals, and various forms of nature
- Mysticism, a sense of openness to things that are not literally provable.

Those who tend to be identified as spiritual score much higher on the index of self-transcendence than persons who are lower on the spiritual continuum (Kluger, 2004). Individuals scoring high in self-transcendence have a powerful sense of connectedness among people, places, and things. Those who are lower on the scale tend to emphasize discrepancies and differences rather than similarities and interrelationships. It should be noted that a gender difference does exist on this scale. Women, independent of other variables such as race or nationality, consistently score significantly higher than men on the attribute of self-transcendence.

The biosocial model examines the underlying neurobiological and cultural bases of individual difference (Cloninger, 1994). Subsequent neuropharmacological and neurobehavioral studies have traced which brain chemicals are released and which structures are activated when selected traits are exhibited.

Central to the biosocial model was the use of studies of both identical and fraternal twins, families, and adoptions to determine which of selected traits are more genetic and which are more environmental. Twin studies indicate that spirituality (as measured by the self-transcendence attribute) is not culturally based. That is, children do not learn to be spiritual from their parents, religious leaders, teachers, or other society functions. Perhaps William James hit the nail on the head when he observed: spirituality comes from within, part of a person's genetic wiring. Religiousness, as measured by attributes such as church attendance, is learned in the classical sense from environmental forces; however, spirituality is more innate. Nevertheless, just because a person has a predisposition to be spiritual does not mean that the trait does not need to be cultivated.

Science and Religion

An understanding of the science of divinity involves correlates among cognitive process, physiological behavior, and symbolic cultural expressions (Damasio, 1994). Making sense of the concept of God entails the exploration of both the physical and personal simultaneously. The notion of "making sense" draws on both symbolic thought and the brain apparatus for processing that thought. Albright and Ashbrook (2001) contend that neither the mind nor body alone makes sense by itself.

The ongoing battle between science and religion typically takes center stage regarding the debate over creationism versus evolution. Those strongly in favor of the science perspective believe that religion is a sign of bias and lack of objectivity. For example, many scientists believe that evolution is sufficient to explain life without a deity. As a field, science is anchored by observation, experimentation, and replication. The hallmark of religion is faith that does not mandate tangible evidence but does use it.

Today we are seeing both theologians and scientists bridging the crevasse between the two domains. For example, the Tennessee-born financier John Marks Templeton created the Templeton Foundation to support scientific research, academic courses, and scholarly articles and conferences that result from the cooperative interaction of science and religion.

Theologians such as Albright and Ashbrook (2001) believe that faith takes on new clarity when we are educated by the knowledge of how the brain works to make sense of religion and God. Correspondingly, Hamer (2004) offers us the belief that new discoveries in behavioral genetics and neurobiology show that humans inherit a set of predispositions that make it either easier or more difficult to embrace a higher power. He posits that this inclination toward spirituality is in good measure attributed to our genes. As a geneticist, he attempts to bridge the gap between religion and science. (For a more comprehensive examination of the topic, see Hamer's [2004] *The God Gene: How Faith Is Hardwired into Our Genes* and Albright and Ashbrook's [2001] *Where God Lives in the Human Brain.*)

Role of DNA

Of the thirty-five thousand genes present in the human genome, scientists have identified the function of only about one-third of them. Fortunately, they can now identify sequences of DNA involved in spirituality through differences observed from one individual to the next. All humans have a capacity for spirituality; however, some have more or less than others.

Pharmacologically, no known drugs directly influence spirituality, but several seem to, at least minimally, enhance or mimic states of consciousness at the core of mysticism and self-transcendence. Typically these drugs act on the monoamines more commonly known as the brain chemicals serotonin and dopamine. Hamer (2004) found a clear association between a selected gene polymorphism or combination and self-transcendence. The information carried by DNA is derived from the order of the bases. Hamer (2004) explains that every three bases specify one amino acid, which is the building block of a molecule called protein. Even though an amino acid may contain the same three bases, the order of the bases will produce different forms of amino acid. Twenty different amino acids determine the structure of proteins, the critical players in all biological activity.

The polymorphism A33050C, a single base, can be either an A (adenine) or a C (cytosine) nucleotide. The location of this polymorphism is on the human genome sequence of chromosome 10. Research participants with a C in their DNA on either one or both chromosomes scored significantly higher on self-transcendence than those with an A. Individuals with a C represented 28 percent of the sample whereas 72 percent had an A. Both the C/C and C/A genotypes showed increased self-transcendence over those with the A/A genotype. Statistically speaking, 47 percent of the sample population was in the higher spirituality group compared with 53 percent in the lower group.

Spirituality and Higher Education

In the United States, we are experiencing a shifting demographic population. Cushner, McClelland, and Safford (2003) observe that the United States is experiencing immigration from non-European countries that now rivals the great immigration from Europe during the early part of the twentieth century. This immigration pattern is leading to appreciably greater diversity in our student populations from preschool through college. An understanding of religion and spirituality is salient to understanding the variables of this increased multiculturalism. In addition, world terrorism in the name of religion mandates that we as a society explore and comprehend issues of diversity.

The spiritual dimension in higher education is embedded in every discipline. Palmer (2003) points out that the human quest for connectedness is at the heart of nearly every aspect of the curriculum. He further indicates that we can evoke the spirituality of academia by teaching in ways that permit the "big story" of the discipline to intersect with the "little story" of the student's life. This sense of connectedness and interrelationships is at the heart of constructivist learning.

For individual university students, Palmer (2003) emphasizes that compulsive or reckless behavior, substance abuse, and excessive meaningless sexual encounters partially result from students attempting to escape the pain of inner emptiness. This emptiness can manifest itself in the classroom as a lack of self-discipline, lack of compassion, lack of interest, and lack of self-worth. Does a connection exist between spirituality and student self-satisfaction? According to Hofius (2004), research conducted at the University of California, Los Angeles's Higher Education Research Institute indicates that being religious or spiritual contributes to students' sense of psychological well-being.

Conclusion

We in higher education need to appreciate the value and virtue of the spiritual dimension and the potential for value-added aspects of life for our students. Unconscious and misguided attempts by students to attain some sense of fulfillment can result in varying degrees of addictive behavior. This behavior makes teaching and learning infinitely more difficult. Palmer (2003) asserts, "A spiritualized curriculum values physical, mental, spiritual knowledge and skills. It presents knowledge within cultural and temporal contests, rather than as facts to be memorized or dogma to be followed. It is integrative across all disciplines emphasizing inter-relationships and inter-connectedness.

It challenges students to find their own place in space and time, and to reach for the highest aspirations of the human spirit" (p. 1).

Hamer (2004) concludes that spirituality has a complicated genetic component that has evolved for a purpose. Science has produced evidence that spirituality is beneficial to physical and mental health. Although our genes predispose us to believe, they do not direct us about what to believe. Higher education has a significant role in helping individuals distinguish between beliefs and the act of believing. This understanding has implications for personal well-being and international cross-cultural cohesiveness.

References

Albright, C. R., and Ashbrook, J. B. *Where God Lives in the Human Brain.* Naperville, Ill.: Sourcebooks, 2001.

Burkhardt, M. A. "Spirituality: An Analysis of the Concept." *Holistic Nursing Practice,* 1989, 3(3), 69–77.

Campbell, L. H. "The Spiritual Lives of Artists/Teachers." Paper presented at the annual meeting of the American Educational Research Association, Chicago, Apr. 2003.

Chalmers, D. J. *The Conscious Mind: In Search of a Fundamental Theory.* Oxford, U.K.: Oxford University Press, 1997.

Cloninger, C. R. "Temperament and Personality." *Current Opinion in Neurobiology,* 1994, 4, 266–273.

Cushner, K. H., McClelland, A., and Safford, P. *Human Diversity in Education: An Integrative Approach.* (4th ed.) New York: McGraw-Hill, 2003.

Damasio, A. R. *Descartes' Error: Emotion, Reason, and the Human Brain.* New York: Grossett/Putnam, 1994.

Edelman, G. M. *Bright Air, Brilliant Fire.* New York: Basic Books, 1992.

Hamer, D. *The God Gene: How Faith Is Hardwired into Our Genes.* New York: Doubleday, 2004.

Hofius, S. "A Spiritually Inclined Student Is a Happier Student." *USAToday.com,* Oct. 28, 2004.

Kluger, J. "Is God in Our Genes?" *Time,* Oct. 25, 2004, pp. 62–72.

Narayanasamy, A. "ASSET: A Model for Actioning Spirituality and Spiritual Care Education and Training in Nursing." *Nursing Education Today,* 1999, 19(4), 274–285.

Palmer, P. J. "Teaching with Heart and Soul: Reflections on Spirituality in Teacher Education." *Journal of Teacher Education,* 2003, 54(5), 376–385.

Pargament, K. I., and others. "The Many Meanings of Religiousness: A Policy Capturing Approach." *Journal of Personality,* 1995, 63(4), 953–983.

Zinnbauer, B. J., and others. "Religion and Spirituality: Unfuzzying the Fuzzy." *Journal for the Scientific Study of Religion,* 1997, 36(4), 549–564.

THOMAS J. BUTTERY *is dean of the College of Professional Programs and Social Sciences at Austin Peay State University in Clarksville, Tennessee.*

PHILIP S. ROBERSON *is director of the School of Education at Austin Peay State University in Clarksville, Tennessee.*

6

Faculty concerns, needs, and struggles in relationship to their own spirituality play out in all aspects of their roles as instructors, advisers, and mentors.

Faculty Perspective on Spirituality, Teaching, and Learning on a Nonsectarian Campus: Gleanings from a Book Group

Miriam Rosalyn Diamond

What role does spirituality play in the work of faculty at a nonsectarian university? How can conversations on this topic get started in this setting? And what is the impact of such discussions?

These questions prompted the introduction of a book group on spiritual aspects of teaching and learning at Northeastern University (Boston) in Fall 2001, a project that four years later is going strong. Group goals are to foster connections among colleagues across the university while exploring spiritual aspects of learning and teaching. We aim to create a space where members can reflect how and why they teach as well as new ways they can approach their work. Participants indicate they want to gain a better understanding of "spirituality" and to learn language that will help them view their vocation differently.

Spirituality as It Relates to Teaching

Nonsectarian research institutions emphasize intellectual development and activities among professors. Faculty are expected to analyze, debate, clarify, synthesize, conceptualize, argue, evaluate, hypothesize, propose, and test.

The author thanks all book group participants for their thoughtful insights, stimulating ideas, and the enthusiasm that made this program an ongoing success.

New Directions for Teaching and Learning, no. 104, Winter 2005 © Wiley Periodicals, Inc.

43

We are supposed to be invincible, or at least appear that way to our colleagues and students.

And yet, we are more. We are more than our listing of publications and discoveries. We are more than the number of conferences where we have presented papers and the grants we received. Just as our students are more than their latest grade (and sometimes need to be reminded of that), we are multidimensional. Taking time to view our teaching through a spiritual lens can affirm our holism.

The work we do has the potential to influence multiple dimensions of student life and activity as well. We can provide learners with methods of analyzing literary characters, and we can encourage them to care about others. We can increase their awareness about considerations in designing buildings, and we can teach them to improve the global environment. We can help them conceptualize political models, and we can model how to cope with tragedy. We can teach students to perform calculations, and we can help them feel that they each count, even on a large impersonal campus. Our ideas about the big picture and what is meaningful in life can give us direction on how to approach our classes and where we choose to take them.

We can pursue the possibility that our teaching and interactions with students have ramifications that extend beyond the course. There are those who believe a moral responsibility comes with this work; they yearn to explore what that responsibility is and what the implications are. Some want to consider the belief that our efforts as educators draw from a larger force or power. Teaching can be a sacred undertaking, one that has the power to touch and transform lives. Some view this as a mission, others as a gift. These are among the motivators that bring faculty together from across the university for ninety minutes every two weeks to ponder, question, share, and absorb.

Group Structure and Process

Each term, up to a dozen faculty enroll in and attend the book group meetings. Several people choose to rejoin the group every year while others cycle off, allowing space for new members and, hence, perspectives.

About thirty-five people have taken part in this offering over the past four years. Participants represent a range of disciplines. The group is diverse in other ways, such as age, race, sex, and sexual orientation. Religious and spiritual associations vary, including people who view themselves as spiritual without identifying with a particular religion. Some never disclose their religious or spiritual identification.

The group meets twice monthly, focusing on one book chapter in each session. Discussion leadership rotates. Readings have included Parker Palmer's *The Courage to Teach* (1998), Steven Glazer's *The Heart of Learning* (1999), and *Education as Transformation* by Victor Kazanjian and Peter Laurence (2002). Discussions are question-centered, which opens up conversation and fosters listening and reflection among people from different backgrounds.

Topics That Arise in Discussion

The books catalyze discussion on many themes. Several subject areas can be identified that relate to our role as educators in this diverse setting. Many ideas are sparked by the readings. Key themes can be identified. Because our goal is exploration and the discussions are inquiry-driven, we raise more questions than answers. As with our spiritual beliefs, some questions are never fully answered. Our purpose is to tease out and examine the issues while sharing perspectives and experiences. It is up to each of us to reflect on our own ways to find a resolution—or a path toward resolution. Recurring topics include our relationships with learners, issues around identity and diversity, what we view as our own roles and responsibilities, and the larger culture in which we work.

Creating Holistic Connections and Relationships with Students. We ask whether it is our role to help students find meaning in their lives, and if so, how to do so. Some of us would like to reduce learners' feelings of isolation. Learning each person's name—even in large lecture classes—is one way. If students feel significant, that they matter, they are more likely to be engaged in the learning process. One group member asks students an "unexpected question" about their passions. Another professor talks about the fact that some students want to remain anonymous, not wanting the professors to know their names, to know or see who they are. What kind of impersonal experience is learning when this is their preferred way of being? We are concerned about what this says about our society and our university.

We deliberate whether we do enough to nurture the whole person. Many classes teach students from the "head up." Some participants think room exists for emotions, hopes, concerns, and disappointments in the classroom and that students can be encouraged to express these. Others are convinced this is not the role of educators.

We look at bringing out the core qualities in each student. How can we do this with ones we find difficult to connect with? We ponder ways to inspire them to open up. Someone suggests that trust—of self and of students—is an issue. Others talk about the professor's role in revealing information about himself or herself as a person. Someone raises a question about the function of hope.

We mull over cultivating compassion toward students who do not seem to assume their part of the deal, who do not follow through. We can try to reach out, find out what is going on for them. One member wonders how much we actually do for our students. She sees an analogy with garden flowers who grew "in spite of, not because of" her. She feels similarly about learners in her classroom.

A participant points out that when students make us feel uneasy, this is a clue to increase our awareness of something in ourselves. At the same time, not all students like us. This is a struggle with which a number of us identify. For many of us, positive relationships are the groundwork for learning. Yet, there is so much in each student's life and history that may influence how he or she views us and how each student sees learning.

How can we heal them? One person says we can try to heal the baggage that students bring with them: fear of the subject or low self-confidence. We can provide tools for them to heal themselves and to improve their ability to communicate who they are and what they think. We can help them to be present and to feel that the different aspects of themselves are in harmony. We can help them acknowledge transitions in their days, even the transition into our classroom, by introducing activities that help them shift (writing, reflection, acknowledging each others' presence) before plunging into course material.

Another path to healing may occur through positive reinforcement. Our students have been critiqued so much. We can reassure them that they are on a right path, that they are okay. One participant encourages students to state for themselves what they do well. We deliberate on the notion that faculty can create hope for jaded and hurt students, a daunting responsibility, but an important one.

Identity and Diversity. One participant discovered that students with stronger spiritual beliefs are more likely to define themselves "from the inside out." These people let the external aspects of who they are (including illness and disability) have less influence on their self-image. We look at helping our students realize positive identities, noting that many (particularly those who do not identify as belonging to "minority" groups) define themselves by what they are not, rather than who they are. This leads to the bigger question: "Who am I?" Can it be answered *without* reference to our connection to others?

One group member asks, "Am I my hand? My body? My mind?" He feels that we are our souls. A psychology professor tells us she encourages students to connect with their clients' souls, who they are, what they are suffering, what brought them to therapy. She wants them to create a space for that spiritual bond in the relationship.

We contemplate our role in helping students hear their callings. If this is part of our charge, how do we go about fulfilling it? Some mention the importance of listening and coaching in this process. Others create safe spaces to explore, modeling by showing how they followed their own callings, and give students permission to explore.

The next step is building connections. Dealing with others leads us to examine how diversity emerges in our work. This is a messy topic for many. A spiritual framework can help us define who we are and how we relate to people. For example, we want students to value the notion that several truths can exist simultaneously.

Challenges are involved in addressing diversity with our students as part of our courses. A tension exists between being concerned about offending students and wanting to acknowledge differences. *Really* talking about diversity in class may raise uneasy emotions, such as anger and pain.

Feelings may get hurt. Even so, several group members feel the need to deal with this issue.

The group debates whether conversations on difference and spirituality should mark and respect boundaries or work toward transcending them. One member suggests that focusing on experience, rather than belief, unites people. Another articulates that although boundaries should not be the emphasis, every so often we find ourselves colliding with them. We note how the characterization of those boundaries can differ based on the beliefs, practices, and majority-minority status of discussants involved.

Professors' Role and Responsibility. We contemplate the function of love in our work. Some members profess a love for their discipline. Others express love of learning and teaching and try to inspire this in students. A number of participants love particular approaches or methods of teaching, whereas others love the outcome: watching students develop as people. One person points out that love has ups and downs, including dry spells. This can also be said about love of teaching.

We deliberate on the boundaries of our responsibility. A debate arises on whether we should teach values. Our principles are often closely connected to our spiritual beliefs. Given this, do we need to strive for common values in our society or develop ethics among our students? We ask if it is enough to model but not "teach" or impose values. We consider cultivating student awareness of the effect of their actions on others and the environment. For many of us, this self-environment interaction is a component of our faith.

Some of us focus on creating safe spaces—for exploration, deliberation, expression—in our classrooms. We can do this by following our group's model: establishing ground rules and norms for participation, active listening, respect, and disagreement. We can teach students to engage each other through questions, rather than statements. We can demonstrate how and why to value different perspectives and ways of mining for more information when a student seems incorrect or misinformed.

On the other hand, some book group participants prefer to push students beyond their zones of comfort. Life requires people to step outside habitual, protected spaces and move into the unknown. That is the place where real learning may occur. Students can learn to navigate the wilderness, to deal with the unfamiliar. The group debates whether our goal is to nurture or to push students. In the end, we wonder if we can do both: build spaces within which it feels safe for students to explore areas of discomfort.

We acknowledge our responsibilities to ourselves, such as the need to be at peace with ourselves before we can be at peace in the classroom. Most of us feel compelled to develop and articulate our own perspectives on spirituality before we can raise these issues in the classroom. Too often, we tend to get caught up in multiple short-term demands, losing the big picture, the deeper meanings, the long-term goals in our lives. One member suggests that reflection can be the antidote to depletion. Sometimes we simply feel too exhausted to reflect. We dare ourselves to set aside time to do nothing. Can we make space for that, given the demands of university life? And in turn, can we encourage students to do the same?

Environment in Which We Teach. We explore how our society in general and education in particular tend to emphasize product and appearance, rather than process. This is reflected in the way students seem more focused on grades than on learning. Our culture sets this up from the start of each person's education. We are concerned that something important gets lost through the emphasis on scientific testing and documentation of everything we do. Even the engineers in our circle say there should be room for the unseen to enter an equation, that not all phenomena can be explained by science alone.

We again talk about allowing space for reflection and prioritization in learning. How else will citizens of the world develop their own values and standards for assessing what is important in this consumeristic (one person calls it "disposable") culture? There seems to be a hesitation to explore things deeply in our society, and we want to remedy that in our classes.

At the same time, a growing desire evolves for active involvement in groups. We see it in increased congregant participation in organized religious settings, mirroring the movement toward active learning and away from the hierarchical classroom. New technologies may influence this shift. Perhaps the recent popularity of book groups is another example of this phenomenon.

These are some of the topics that arise. These discussions do not end at the book group door, however. Apparently, neither does their impact.

Consequences of Book Group Participation

Participant feedback reveals that participation in the group affects teaching, in addition to creating connections among participants. A professor shares excerpts from our book with her students. Several members indicate that by taking turns leading discussion, the group has allowed them to develop and hone skills in encouraging and moderating discourse, often on topics that are disquieting. As a result of the group, members report a deeper appreciation for the role of spirituality in their work and increased professional confidence. A number mention that they now do more reflection and writing.

Participants state that this program increases their awareness of students' concerns and makes them more mindful of the influence they have on learners. It alerts them to the sacred qualities these exchanges can assume with effects that ripple beyond the time and place of the interaction. A number of faculty indicate that their involvement in the group has given them courage to address spiritual matters in their own classes. Some find themselves interacting with students in new ways, as whole people or as colleagues on a journey together.

In her essay entitled "The Heart of Learning—Reflections of a Book Group Member," participant Susan Pilaud states, "I found that sharing with others strengthened my awareness of obstacles teachers and students face and encouraged me to reach out to my students in a deeper, more compassionate way. . . . The Spiritual Aspects of Teaching book group raises consciousness of the more human yet intangible qualities of learning that we cannot forget. . . . In the midst of our successes, we in academia must not neglect tending to the heart" (2003, pp. 10–11).

Conclusion

A book group on spiritual aspects of teaching and learning provides the space many faculty members in a nonsectarian setting crave so that they can reflect on their work. It also offers the opportunity to express aspects of themselves often unrecognized in their daily routine.

Faculty welcome the chance to meet and connect with colleagues from other corners of the university. Through their involvement in this group, professors come to articulate and to value the sacredness of their profession. It is clear that the impact of the spirituality book club extends beyond the perimeter of the group itself.

References

Glazer, S. (ed.). *The Heart of Learning: Spirituality in Education.* New York: Tarcher, 1999.

Kazanjian, V. H., and Laurence, P. L. (eds.). *Education as Transformation: Religious Pluralism, Spirituality, and a New Vision for Higher Education in America.* New York: Lang, 2002.

Palmer, P. J. *The Courage to Teach: Exploring the Inner Landscape of a Teacher's Life.* San Francisco: Jossey-Bass, 1998.

Pilaud, S. "The Heart of Learning—Reflections of a Book Group Member." *Teaching Matters,* 2003, *8*(4), 9–11. Available at: http://www.ceut.neu.edu/publications.htm. Accessed Oct. 3, 2004.

MIRIAM ROSALYN DIAMOND *is associate director of Northeastern University's Center for Effective University Teaching and coauthor of* Chalk Talk: E-Advice from Jonas Chalk, Legendary College Teacher *(New Forums Press, 2004).*

7

Curriculum concepts successfully used to teach third-year medical students about spirituality in health care can be readily adapted for use in any professional or preprofessional health curriculum.

A Modular Curriculum for Integrating Spirituality and Health Care

Allen L. Pelletier, John W. McCall

Paul Gauguin, the French Impressionist painter, left as his masterpiece a large mural titled "Triptych." Three Tahitian village scenes progress across the canvas from birth to middle age to senescence and death. Inscribed in the upper left-hand corner are these lines, translated, "Where did we come from? What are we? Where are we going?" These profound questions that express the ancient yearnings of humanity have been addressed by religious and spiritual traditions for countless centuries.

Practitioners of the "healing arts" deal daily with Gauguin's three universal questions. Today, we have an array of impressive technology that can extend life—but at what cost to our common humanity? How do we train a generation of future health care professionals to draw on the best of science and the rich insights of spirituality and religious tradition, without doing violence to either?

Spirituality, Health, and Wellness

We take as our starting point the premise that every individual (at some level) seeks transcendence, that is, both personal connection with a higher power and intrapersonal development of the self. Coyle (2002) defines *spirituality* as a felt connection to one's deepest values, principles, and beliefs. This is the framework that provides meaning and purpose in the face of illness. These values may be explicitly religious in expression, but are not necessarily so.

When someone is ill, he or she often begins consciously asking, perhaps for the first time, one or more of the three universal questions posed by

NEW DIRECTIONS FOR TEACHING AND LEARNING, no. 104, Winter 2005 © Wiley Periodicals, Inc.

Gauguin. Our educational model attempts to link the universal need for transcendence (spirituality broadly defined, connection with a higher power and self-actualization) and the felt needs that often surface in the crisis of ill health.

We maintain that a model applied only to the experience of illness is incomplete. Our educational model points to the possibility of true "wellness" in the connection of body-mind-spirit. It is easy to lose sight of this experience of wholeness and wellness in the reductionistic, scientific, highly specialized biomedical model of medical education.

A Brief Overview of the Health-Education Process

Graduate-level health education is usually divided into preclinical (basic sciences) and clinical courses. In the clinical curricula, students begin to see patients and actively participate in their care with progressive levels of involvement and responsibility. Clinical training by its nature is experiential and "hands on." Didactic lectures, seminars, and small group discussion during clinical training blocks focus on teaching technical skills or imparting information that is immediately practical and relevant in the care of patients.

This pattern of training has important implications for curricular development and determining when subjects are best introduced. We shall explore this idea in the following sections.

Spirituality in the Clinical Arena

Studies consistently demonstrate that most patients want to talk about spiritual concerns with their health care provider, yet few providers do so (Barnes, Plotnikoff, Fox, and Pendleton, 2000; Ellis, Vinson, and Ewigman, 1999; Maugans and Wadland, 1991). Many health care providers report feeling ill equipped and inadequate to discuss spiritual matters with their patients (Barnes, Plotnikoff, Fox, and Pendleton, 2000; Ellis, Vinson, and Ewigman, 1999). In an attempt to address these concerns, eighty-four U.S. medical schools now offer at least some formal course work in spirituality and health (Fortin and Barnett, 2004).

Evaluation of spirituality teaching in professional schools is lacking. We do not know for certain the ideal time in the curriculum to introduce these concepts. We have chosen to introduce our spirituality curriculum during a clinical rotation, where the information is immediately practical and relevant to patient care.

Focus: A Five-Hour Module on Spirituality and Health for Third-Year Medical Students

The University of Tennessee College of Medicine, like most medical schools, has a required clinical rotation in family medicine. Our particular clerkship is eight weeks long, during the third year of medical training. During these eight weeks, students work with and are mentored by family medicine specialists in a variety of inpatient and outpatient settings.

During this block, students attend a required five-hour module relating concepts of spirituality to health and the clinical care of patients. We use a multimodality approach described in the next section. Assigned readings are provided in advance of the seminar (Borrell-Carrio, Suchman, and Epstein, 2004; Daaleman, 2004; McCord and others, 2004; Scheurich, 2003). Students are expected to discuss these readings during the small group sessions.

Core Principles: ArkWings Model

We began this chapter with Gauguin's "three life questions." In 1991, one of us (J.W.McC.) conceptualized an integrated model for health and well-being called ArkWings, using Gauguin's three questions as a starting point (McCall and others, 2002). At the core of the model is the concept that health is more than the mere absence of illness. Rather, it is living life "well" in relationship to the triad of God-neighbor-self, each of which can be related in turn to the three "universal questions" of life (Figure 7.1).

The ArkWings model is "perspectival." Each universal question is one perspective or lens that allows us to focus on one particular aspect of health and wellness. The whole can be entered and explored from any side of the triangle. Although ArkWings has a faith-based component, it is nonallied, nondenominational, and multicultural.

Outline of the Spirituality and Health Module

As explained below, the module is composed of two required sessions and one optional session.

Session I (one hour fifteen minutes). The first session begins with a pretest survey of the students that assesses their attitudes, beliefs, and behaviors regarding spirituality (Exhibit 7.1). This takes about ten minutes. We distribute background readings and current journal articles that discuss spirituality in health care. These will be used in the second session.

In the first session, we introduce the core ideas of integral (or holistic) medicine: a patient-centered approach that takes seriously the whole person as a mind-body-spirit unity. A video titled "Consciousness and Healing: Integral Approaches to Mind-Body Medicine" (Schlitz, Amorok, and Micozzi, 2004) describes these concepts in detail. The video is about fifty minutes long.

We close the first session by grouping students for later discussion of the video and assigned readings. Volunteer student facilitators are chosen in advance to lead the small groups.

Session II (two hours forty-five minutes). We present the ArkWings core concept model and discuss the interrelationship of health and illness

Figure 7.1. The ArkWings Wellness Model

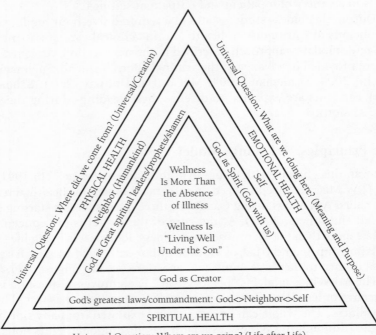

Note: This model visually demonstrates the relationship among Gauguin's "three life questions," spirituality, and health. The Trinity Effect: the components of each triangle are interconnected to all other components in such a way that the whole becomes greater than the sum of its parts (science and faith). ArkWings is a registered trademark of John W. McCall, 2004. The diagram is used by his permission.

in all dimensions of the person (mind-body-spirit). The small groups, led by student facilitators, discuss Gauguin's three life questions, the video, and the assigned readings. After small group discussion, we review student pretest results.

At this point, we reconvene and introduce approaches to obtaining a spiritual inventory (or "spiritual history") in the clinical setting (Anandarajah and Hight, 2002; Maugans and Wadland, 1991; Puchalski and Romer, 2000).

We follow with two short videos that tie this information together through case presentations: a documentary film, "Stanley" (Aachtenberg and Mitchell, 2002), that deals sensitively with spiritual issues in end-of-life care, followed by a summary video, "Give Me Strength" (Johns Hopkins University, 2001). We discuss the videos and all the seminar material with the entire group. The discussion sometimes becomes animated and lively at this point! We conclude with a post-test and module evaluation. The post-test and wrap-up take about fifteen minutes.

Exhibit 7.1. Spirituality and Health Family Medicine Clerkship Survey

Please respond to each statement by checking the response that best describes your attitude or behavior. **Do not place any personal identifiers on this form.** Today's date: _____

	Strongly Agree	Agree	Disagree	Strongly Disagree
1. Faith and science are becoming more closely linked	( )	( )	( )	( )
2. What is your attitude about the following quote: "All cures are temporary, but healing is divine"?	( )	( )	( )	( )
3. I believe one's faith or spirituality can affect:				
A. Physical health	( )	( )	( )	( )
B. Emotional health	( )	( )	( )	( )
C. Spiritual health	( )	( )	( )	( )
4. Faith or spirituality plays an important role in my life	( )	( )	( )	( )
5. I practice my faith or spirituality in a group through a community of faith on a regular basis	( )	( )	( )	( )
6. I would be willing to discuss issues of faith or spirituality with my patients, if they expressed an interest or desire	( )	( )	( )	( )
7. I would be willing to pray with a patient who asked me to	( )	( )	( )	( )
8. I would be comfortable in doing Nos. 6 and 7	( )	( )	( )	( )
9. When appropriate, I plan on making matters of faith or spirituality a conscious part of my clinical practice	( )	( )	( )	( )
10. I am interested in making international medical missions a part of my clinical practice	( )	( )	( )	( )
11. Spirituality and Health as a topic is adequately covered in the medical school curriculum	( )	( )	( )	( )
12. I have adequate knowledge concerning the various issues related to the topic Spirituality and Health	( )	( )	( )	( )

    A. What community of faith do you belong to?_____

      Examples: none, Christian, Jewish, Muslim, Hindu, Buddhist, etc.

    B. Sex: ( ) Female ( ) Male

Session III (optional noon lunch session). We show a video by Larry Dossey, "Healing Prayer" (date not available), followed by facilitated discussion. Participation in this session is not required, but a significant number of the students do participate.

Evaluation of the Module

Our teaching process is being continually refined. Our pretest data suggest that up to this point in their education, most students feel ill equipped to deal with patients' spiritual concerns. Based on our post-test survey, there is an increasing level of comfort with spirituality in the clinical setting after the seminar. After the seminar, many of the students express interest in additional discussion and training to continue to integrate spirituality and wellness concepts into their medical practice (McCall and others, 2005).

Evolution of Spirituality Education at the University of Tennessee College of Medicine

In the future, we hope to integrate spirituality education longitudinally across the four-year medical school curriculum. One program we are investigating is "The Healer's Art," developed by Rachel Naomi Remen at the University of California-San Francisco School of Medicine. "The Healer's Art" is offered at about thirty medical schools in the United States and Canada, with plans to adapt it for use in schools of nursing, pharmacy, and allied health professions. Based on the post-test results of student interest, we also plan to develop a fourth-year elective rotation that will integrate spirituality and bioethics in the clinical setting.

Application to Other Professional Health Care Courses

All health professionals deal with spiritual concerns daily in their practice. Gauguin's three universal questions as conceptualized in the ArkWings Model transcend all health care disciplines, cultures, and faiths.

Our five-hour module could be easily adapted, in whole or in part, to teach spirituality and wellness concepts to any health professional student. The videos we show, particularly the documentary "Stanley," are highly relevant to nursing, dental, pharmacy, and allied health professional students as well as to medical students. A teacher would need only to direct the discussion toward applications in his or her particular health care field. Many of the concepts outlined here could be profitably integrated into preprofessional courses in psychology, sociology, ethics, anthropology, or religion.

Conclusion

Medical education has come full circle from the days when the roles of the physician and priest or shaman were seen as complementary. Medical educators increasingly acknowledge that spiritual yearnings and the search for meaning are part of the human condition, with inseparable connections to health and the experience of illness. Medicine that is truly holistic has always taken the spiritual dimension of persons into account. The five-hour clinical training module presented in this chapter is one tested approach to introducing spirituality into the health professional curriculum. The principles and techniques described have potential for broad application to all fields of professional health education.

Some things do not change. The role of the health professional is, and remains, "to heal and cure sometimes; to comfort always." Our challenge as educators is to help students discover and embrace this ancient and time-honored role.

References

Aachtenberg, B., and Mitchell, C. *Stanley.* Boston: Fanlight Productions, 2002. Videotape.

Anandarajah, G., and Hight, E. "Spirituality and Medical Practice: Using the HOPE Questions as a Practical Tool for Spiritual Assessment." *American Family Physician,* 2002, *63(1),* 81–89.

Barnes, L. L., Plotnikoff, G. A., Fox, K., and Pendleton, S. "Spirituality, Religion, and Pediatrics: Intersecting Worlds of Healing." *Pediatrics,* 2000, *106*(4 Suppl), 899–908.

Borrell-Carrio, F., Suchman, A. L., and Epstein, R. M. "The Biopsychosocial Model 25 Years Later: Principles, Practice, and Scientific Inquiry." *Annals of Family Medicine,* 2004, *2*(6), 576–582.

Coyle, J. "Spirituality and Health: Towards a Framework for Exploring the Relationship Between Spirituality and Health." *Journal of Advanced Nursing,* 2002, *37*(6), 589–597.

Daaleman, T. "Religion, Spirituality, and the Practice of Medicine." *Journal of the American Board of Family Practice,* 2004, *17*(5), 370–376.

Dossey, L. "Healing Prayer." Copy donated to Mary Baker Eddy Library by L. Dossey, no date or copyright information available. DVD.

Ellis, M. R., Vinson, D. C., and Ewigman, B. "Addressing Spiritual Concerns of Patients: Family Physicians' Attitudes and Practices." *Journal of Family Practice,* 1999, *48*(2), 105–109.

Fortin, A. H. 6th, and Barnett, K. G. "STUDENTJAMA. Medical School Curricula in Spirituality and Medicine." *Journal of the American Medical Association,* 2004, *291*(23), 2883.

Johns Hopkins University. *Give Me Strength–Spirituality in the Medical Encounter.* Baltimore: Johns Hopkins University, 2001. Videotape.

Maugans, T. A., and Wadland, W. C. "Religion and Family Medicine: A Survey of Physicians and Patients." *Journal of Family Practice,* 1991, *32*(2), 210–213.

McCall, J. W., Delzell, J., and others. "Adventure Wellness Retreats: Balancing Personal and Professional Life." Paper presented at the American Medical Association and Canadian Medical Association International Conference on Physician Health. Vancouver, B.C., Canada, Oct. 2002.

McCall, J. W., Walker, R., and others. "Spirituality in Health Care: Attitude and Beliefs Among Medical Students in a Required Family Medicine Clerkship Curriculum." Poster presented at the 31st Annual Predoctoral Education Conference, Jan. 28, 2005, Albuquerque.

McCord, G., and others. "Discussing Spirituality with Patients: A Rational and Ethical Approach." *Annals of Family Medicine,* 2004, *2*(4), 356–361.

Puchalski, C., and Romer, A. L. "Taking a Spiritual History Allows Clinicians to Understand Patients More Fully." *Journal of Palliative Medicine,* 2000, *3*(1), 129–137.

Scheurich, N. "Reconsidering Spirituality and Medicine." *Academic Medicine,* 2003, *78*(4), 356–360.

Schlitz, M., Amorok, T., and Micozzi, M. S. *Consciousness and Healing: Integral Approaches to Mind-Body Medicine.* St. Louis: Mosby, 2004. DVD.

University of California-San Francisco School of Medicine. "The Healer's Art." Institute for the study of Health and Wellness at Commonweal. http://www.commonweal.org /ishi/programs/healers_art.html. Accessed Mar. 24, 2004.

ALLEN L. PELLETIER is assistant professor of family medicine at the University of Tennessee College of Medicine, Memphis.

JOHN W. MCCALL is associate professor of family medicine and director of research and faculty development in the Department of Family Medicine at the University of Tennessee College of Medicine, Memphis.

8

*The foundational spiritual truths of sectarian institutions,
often criticized by the secular academy, may provide a
basis for a vigorous search for truth in the transition from
modern to postmodern society.*

Issues Related to Spirituality and the Search for Truth in Sectarian Institutions of Higher Education

Harry Lee Poe

With the advent of what many refer to as a "postmodern" understanding of life and culture has come a renewal of interest in the spiritual dimension of life. For most of the modern period, western thinkers viewed any reference to spirituality as akin to superstition and ignorance. The postmodern mindset, however, has embraced the reality of the spiritual dimension to life. What complicates matters is that modernity is not yet dead and postmodernity is not yet here. We live in a transitional age. Neat distinctions do not exist, and contradictions abound.

Disciplines in the academy like social work, which was long associated with a secular understanding of life, have recognized that spirituality plays an important role in what it means to be human. In fact, social work faced the fact that its core value of the dignity and worth of each person could not be sustained on a purely materialistic understanding of life (M. Poe, 2002a, 2002b). The Council on Social Work Education and the social work profession now recognize the significance of the spiritual dimension of life.

It would seem that this renewed recognition of spirituality as a dimension of life would create an openness to the insights of the two-thousand-year-old Christian tradition of education. Unfortunately, the postmodern view of spirituality shuns the Christian view that spirituality has a cognitive and an affective dimension. The insistence on a cognitive element to spiritual experience places a cloud of suspicion over Christian approaches to education. Whereas postmodern spirituality affirms individual spiritual

NEW DIRECTIONS FOR TEACHING AND LEARNING, no. 104, Winter 2005 © Wiley Periodicals, Inc.

experience, it rejects any effort to articulate an integrated meaning to collective spiritual experiences.

In the postmodern context, the term *spirituality* has as imprecise a meaning as postmodernity! From a biblical perspective, the human spirit involves the life force, will, emotions, intellect, character, creativity, and imagination in an interrelated and inseparable relationship. The effort to identify the elements of spirituality, however, may create a false sense of demarcation between these various areas because they actually relate indivisibly to one another as a single, unified whole.

Within the Christian tradition, the spirit has a metaphysical or transcendent dimension by which humans may experience God. Spirituality involves the methods, means, institutions, customs, and practices by which people cultivate their spirits. Christian spirituality has the goal of bringing the human spirit into communion with Christ to experience transformation by the Holy Spirit. The act of faith involves the emotional, intellectual, and volitional response to the cognitive truth claims of faith in union with the spiritual experience of God.

Abandonment of the Pursuit of Truth

The truth claims involved in the Christian understanding of spirituality go against the current fashion of the complete autonomy of the individual in which the individual constructs an independent, self-authenticating belief system that works for the individual. Postmodern spirituality provides an alternative to corporate religion and a commonly held system of core beliefs and values characteristic of any healthy culture. This focus on the individual and subjectivity creates for the postmodern person a world in which truth does not exist. All value judgments are relative. In a postmodern rubric, there is no truth to pursue.

In the twentieth century, the secular critique of sectarian institutions of higher education charged that such schools biased or thwarted the pursuit of truth because of the foundational spiritual truths they affirmed. In the twenty-first century, a postmodern critique of sectarian institutions of higher education charges that such schools thwart education by advocating the existence of objective truth. In short, the faith affirmations of Christian schools and the implications they suggest create conflict for those who do not hold the same faith.

The postmodern mindset with its hodge podge of longings and mutually contradictory ideas will likely prove to be not another epoch like the Middle Ages but another fashion like the Jazz Age (H. Poe, 2001). Nonetheless, its current pervasiveness in the academy suggests that the old secularism of modernity failed to provide a satisfactory philosophical foundation for the modern agenda: the pursuit of truth. The postmodern longing intuitively recognizes its own spiritual nature. Unfortunately, it also has grown addicted to the absence of constraints that truth might impose.

The arts, humanities, and social sciences in the broad academy continue to struggle with the chaos that ensues from the lack of direction that the abandonment of truth imposes. Do the disciplines in the sectarian institutions of higher learning fare any better? Does spirituality rooted in a cognitive faith encourage or discourage the pursuit of truth?

The muzzling of Galileo stands as the standard example of sectarian restrictions on the pursuit of knowledge within the academy. Actually, the case of Galileo demonstrates the problem with the academy rather than with religion. In that age when church, state, and academy formed a seamless society, the modern mind can easily ignore the actual dynamics. Galileo was punished by the academy for rejecting the prevailing Aristotelian understanding of the universe. His views did not conflict with religion but with philosophy. Galileo's contemporary, Sir Francis Bacon, argued that philosophy had a stranglehold on science. Bacon insisted that science could not advance as long as science had to conform to the expectations of the prevailing philosophical interpretations of reality. Neither Galileo nor Bacon regarded faith as the enemy of learning. Rather, they viewed the philosophical commitments of scholars as the most crippling dangers to the academic enterprise.

Spirituality, Beliefs, and Values

Because the human spirit involves intellect, character, creativity, imagination, emotion, and will, in addition to the life force, education attends to the human spirit. In every aspect of what it does, education aims at the development of the human spirit. As a result, education always involves spirituality of some kind even if the articulated version of spirituality denies the existence of the metaphysical or transcendent, such as communism or other forms of materialism. Any belief system goes beyond the material world to ascribe meaning to the world of experience, as communism does with its dialectic. Every educational system is based on some core value or belief system.

The secularists have the same problem as the sectarians. They may not be "religious," but they are spiritual. They have beliefs and values as deeply held as religious beliefs and values, and these beliefs and values frame their intellectual work. The major difference is that religious beliefs and values are held in common by a community that holds itself accountable. The religious beliefs and values have served a beneficial function for a community of believers over time. The publicly held beliefs and values are open to scrutiny, discussion, and reinterpretation.

Ideally, religious beliefs should have some influence on how bankers, physicians, builders, and sales personnel do their work. Likewise, religious beliefs should have some influence on how scholars do their work. Beliefs and values affect how people approach their discipline. The private beliefs and values of the secularist will affect the secularist's scholarship as much as the religious person's beliefs and values should affect his or her scholarship. The difference lies in the personal, idiosyncratic nature of secular belief in contrast to the communal nature of religious belief.

The very issue of quality in education depends on a basis for value, but value is a spiritual quality evaluated by spiritual beings. On what basis can an educational system without a commonly held system of value long strive for quality? The postmodern collapse of value within academic disciplines illustrates the problem. The discipline of history struggles to find its own purpose when it no longer conceives of history as having any meaning. Charles S. Maier, Leverett Saltonstall Professor of History at Harvard, at a lecture given at Union University on October 21, 2003, described the discipline's search for a subject when considering the problem of world history. Likewise, the discipline of literature struggles to find a purpose for itself when it no longer believes that texts have any meaning. Other disciplines have similar problems.

To place the problem in context, consider the difference between the study of literature and the study of physics. Physics underwent a major reconsideration under the influence of Isaac Newton. Two hundred years later, it went through another major reconsideration under the influence of Albert Einstein and Nils Bohr. The study of literature has gone through these major transitions several times a decade since the middle of the twentieth century. The difference between the two disciplines relates to how much of the Christian faith they have retained. Modern science is based on the Christian view that the universe and everything in it actually exists. Science is possible because the universe exists. The study of literature has lost confidence that it has anything to study. In this context, George Marsden (1997) has argued that Christian scholarship has a positive contribution to make to the broad academy because of the foundational faith perspective that gives meaning to academic research.

Suspicions of Faith

To a great extent, the modern academy has fallen prey to the same problem that crippled the academy in the days of Galileo and Bacon. The seamless relationship of church, state, and academy has disappeared, so it is easier to see that the academy is not crippled by religion but by a variety of popularly held philosophical ideas that prevail in the academy. The same problem can occur in a modern sectarian college or university, but it is important to note that the problem is of the same kind as occurs in the secular academy. It is a problem embedded in the academic enterprise, an occupational hazard that can be recognized only by disciplined self-critique. The advantage of the sectarian institution is that it has an independent standard against which to evaluate itself.

Control. One of the great complaints against sectarian education is that religion imposes a control on education. The cognitive claims of faith do provide a control for higher education, but not in the sense its critics suppose. As a control, faith does not restrict knowledge but makes a way for knowledge. Bacon's great legacy to knowledge is the scientific method, which leads to new knowledge. For the experimentation of the scientific method to work, it is necessary to have a norm that provides control for the research. Without the control to establish the standard of normality, the discovery of new knowledge on the path to truth is impossible. Without the presence of a recognized control, only chaos can ensue; thus, faith contributes to the search for truth.

Philosophical Bias. Higher education in the West made such significant strides for two reasons: it became self-critically aware of its tendency to place philosophical ideas above its research, and it had the norm of the Christian faith to provide a constant point of reference. Part of the contemporary crisis in higher education has arisen because of the new philosophical frameworks that various disciplines have incorporated into their thinking in the way that the early medieval world incorporated platonism and the late medieval world incorporated aristotelianism. Another aspect of the crisis in higher education has resulted from the loss of a basis for the unity of knowledge that Christian faith supplied until after World War II.

Sectarian institutions are not free from the danger of adopting a philosophical perspective through which the world is viewed. It was in a Christian context that Bacon pointed out the problem of allowing a philosophical view to prejudice the pursuit of knowledge. Just as imposing Aristotle's philosophy on the world caused science to see the world in a particular way, the imposition of various assumptions and presuppositions on the Bible can cause us to read the Bible in a particular way. Oddly, contemporary theories of literary study do not help us avoid this problem. The reader-response theory of interpretation justifies any reading of Scripture while reinforcing the reader's prejudices.

External Pressures. Intimidation by the prevailing fad, style, attitude, political mood, or popular opinion is always a danger for secular and sectarian schools. In fact, the problem may be more acute in the secular setting where the plurality of pressures is greater. An example of this pressure occurred in the late 1970s when influence was successfully exerted to remove homosexuality from the list of personality disorders and certain other nonpsychotic mental disorders in the *Diagnostic and Statistical Manual of Mental Disorders (DSM-II)*. Government, business, foundations, and special interest groups attempt to exert pressure on secular institutions. Denominations, pastors, and religious groups attempt to apply pressure on sectarian institutions. Being a secular or sectarian institution neither heightens nor decreases the possibility of pressure from external sources that might affect teaching and scholarship. It merely determines the types of groups that might apply pressure.

The secular academy has its counterpart to the denominational body. It was perhaps easier to notice the official decrees of the former Soviet State concerning what constituted legitimate research than to notice these dynamics in the American academy. Within the American academy, education has fast become a commodity in which students have become consumers. Like all other consumer products, the value of disciplines in the secular academy is one of supply and demand. Legitimate research is fast becoming what will benefit the funding corporation or the interests of the majority political party in Congress. Market forces and corporate interests can be a much more virulent form of influence and control in a negative way than denominational ties and faith commitments.

Spiritual Affinity with Higher Education

Not all sectarian educational institutions will meet with the same success in advancing knowledge because they begin with different understandings of reality and different educational aims. The three monotheistic religions hold to a common understanding of God as Creator; therefore, they affirm an objective world that can be studied and known. Each of these religions has subgroups, however, that reject certain areas of progress that have implications for the pursuit of knowledge. Hasidic Jews, Wahhabi Muslims, and Fundamentalist Christians would all have some reservations about the pursuit of knowledge. Mark Noll (1994) has explored some of this dynamic and its impact on evangelical scholarship. Unlike the western religious tradition that is oriented around the concept of deity, the major eastern religions of Hinduism and Buddhism are oriented around the common concept of reincarnation. These religions have under their broad umbrella a variety of concepts of God, but their essential tenet of faith concerns the nature of reality rather than the nature of deity. This difference affects the kinds of concerns of a people and the questions they ask.

Western education departed from paganism under Christianity, which had been influenced by Jewish rabbinic thought. Christian learning influenced the development of the Islamic university through Byzantine Christians. Islamic education then influenced the development of Christian education in the West in the high Middle Ages through the Jewish community. The common understanding of a created, ordered world provided a context for the study of that world. As a result, every discipline of the western academy has a relationship to a central article of Christian faith (H. Poe, 2004). Not all sectarian views will be compatible with the interests of western higher education, which is indelibly stamped with the assumptions of monotheism. Thus, not all sectarian institutions will have the same result when they have "rival" spiritualities with "rival" cognitive truth claims about reality.

Challenge to Sectarian Education

In the vast majority of cases, however, sectarian schools do not offer sectarian education. Most sectarian schools have a nominal relationship to a denomination or religious tradition, but manifestations of spirituality have to do primarily with chapel attendance, codes of conduct, and a required course on religion. James Tunstead Burtchaell (1998) has argued persuasively that a number of factors have led to, as he says in the subtitle of his book, "The Disengagement of Colleges and Universities from Their Christian Churches." Institutions take on a life of their own. The Young Men's Christian Association, founded as an evangelistic organization like the Billy Graham Evangelistic Association, has become the most successful family fitness center in the country while abandoning its primary mission. Schools like Harvard, Yale, Brown, Chicago, and Stanford were founded to advance the gospel, but they have looked to other values of success.

Loyalty to the Guild. Few sectarian schools offer advanced research degrees; therefore, the teachers at sectarian schools earn their doctoral degrees at the great secular universities. As a result, most faculty members of sectarian schools are not taught how to approach their discipline from the perspective of the core beliefs of their faith. The postmodern focus on autonomy and individual values does not diminish the emotional need for recognition and relationships. The danger to sectarian scholarship is the yearning for recognition and acceptance that comes from moving with the crowd. Most faculty members find their identity in their scholarly association at a time when many of the disciplines are struggling for a clear identity.

Poverty and Prosperity. The spirituality of the sectarian institution has a major practical value that many schools did not recognize when they chose to abandon their faith commitments. The poverty of the small, denominational, liberal arts college is legend. Faculty members teach many courses each semester and have little time left for research and writing. The emphasis on teaching and community building leaves little room for scholarship. The challenge for the sectarian school is to increase funding to reduce teaching loads. The schools that have succeeded in this strategy of releasing their faculty members to contribute to their fields of knowledge have largely succeeded because of the recognition in the "market" that the sectarian schools offer more rather than less in the way of intellectual development and the search for truth.

Conclusion

The institutions of a culture have a responsibility for preserving the culture, but the institutions of American life no longer embrace this obligation. Chief among these is higher education. This situation creates confusion for Christians over their role in the academy. Is it to preserve the culture or to speak prophetically to its culture when the rest of the academy is unraveling? At a time when western culture is going through a major period of flux, perhaps the sectarian institutions are in the best position to do both.

References

Burtchaell, J. T. *The Dying of the Light: The Disengagement of Colleges and Universities from Their Christian Churches.* Grand Rapids, Mich.: Eerdmans, 1998.

Diagnostic and Statistical Manual of Mental Disorders. (2nd ed.) Washington, D.C.: American Psychiatric Association, 1968.

Maier, C. S. "What Is a World History a History of? Defining Global History Today." Lecture presented at Union University, Jackson, Tennessee, Oct. 21, 2003.

Marsden, G. *The Outrageous Idea of Christian Scholarship.* New York: Oxford, 1997.

Noll, M. *The Scandal of the Evangelical Mind.* Grand Rapids, Mich.: Eerdmans, 1994.

Poe, H. *Christian Witness in a Postmodern World.* Nashville: Abingdon, 2001.

Poe, H. *Christianity in the Academy.* Grand Rapids, Mich.: Baker, 2004.

Poe, M. "Christian Worldview and Social Work." In D. Dockery and G. Thornbury (eds.), *Shaping a Christian Worldview.* Nashville: Broadman & Holman, 2002a.

Poe, M. "Good News for the Poor: Christian Influences on Social Welfare." In B. Hugen and T. Scales (eds.), *Christianity and Social Work.* (2nd ed.) Botsford, Conn.: North American Association of Christians in Social Work, 2002b.

HARRY LEE POE serves as Charles Colson Professor of Faith and Culture at Union University in Jackson, Tennessee.

9

Engaging spirituality in the workplace is a logical extension of an evolving preworkplace model of individual spirituality.

Preparing Students for Spirituality in the Workplace

Gary D. Geroy

People's sense of spirituality when they enter the world of work is an intrinsic element of their being, evolved and shaped through years of experience and exposure to their environment, and made explicit through their behavior. The spiritual dimension individuals bring to work environments is the sum of the influence of family and peers and interactions with mandated and chosen social structures and systems. Their behaviors are reinforced, corrected, or guided (or all three) by the confluence of several dynamics (Figure 9.1).

The model in Figure 9.1 posits that on a continuum of development through time, spiritual evolution is an outcome of three interactive elements: principal personal growth dynamic, dominant environment, and type of principle guiding social structure.

As with each stage in the evolution of spirituality, individuals entering the workplace likely encounter a cultural mix representing a matrix and synergy of spiritual notions that are new to their previous understandings. These notions may or may not match the values individuals bring to the workplace, such as concern for task process and performance, place of work in life, and the place of individuals in the social construct of work-groups and organization culture.

Understanding these new notions and relating them to the dynamics of previous experience are relevant to successful entry and performance in the workplace. A dominant aspect of this complex undertaking is the reoriented view of spirituality as a functional dimension of performance management in the workplace. As a performance management issue, spirituality

NEW DIRECTIONS FOR TEACHING AND LEARNING, no. 104, Winter 2005 © Wiley Periodicals, Inc.

Figure 9.1. Spiritual Development Factors Continuum

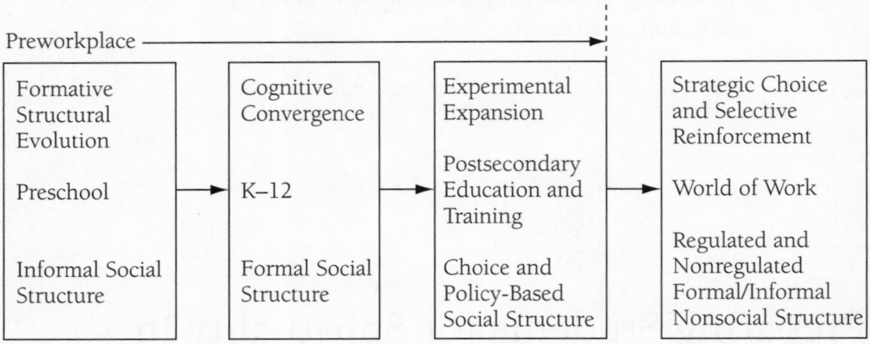

Preworkplace ─────────────────────────────────────►

Formative Structural Evolution	Cognitive Convergence	Experimental Expansion	Strategic Choice and Selective Reinforcement
Preschool	K–12	Postsecondary Education and Training	World of Work
Informal Social Structure	Formal Social Structure	Choice and Policy-Based Social Structure	Regulated and Nonregulated Formal/Informal Nonsocial Structure

is expanded beyond an internal individual force only. Expanding to external aspects, the following section introduces spirituality from various perspectives.

Notion of Spirituality

Literature suggests that individual spirituality transcends religion or professing certain beliefs (Ashmos and Duchon, 2000; Brandt, 1996; Leigh, 1997; Mitroff and Denton, 1999). Rather, spirituality is the internal expression of being, sense of place, interconnectedness, and meaning-seeking.

Spiritual evolution results from transcendental and existential capacity building. Researchers suggest that transcendental capacity is manifested when individuals achieve connection to a network beyond them and foster a sense of community in their environment (Acker, 2000; Ashmos and Duchon, 2000; Mitroff and Denton, 1999). Frankl (1984) attributes existential capacity to an individual emerging from his or her search and gaining meaning and purpose in life. Frankl distinguishes between trying to get meaning *from* life and searching for meaning *in* life. Research suggests that the search for meaning in life entails pursuing the whole person's development, striving for personal goals, and behaving with integrity (Helminiak, 1996; Maslow, 1971). Prehar (2001) suggests three types of commitment behavior as manifestations of spirituality: compliance, affiliation, and internalization. How these evolve is addressed throughout the remainder of this chapter.

Formative Structural Evolution

Until assimilated into the school environment, individuals are influenced primarily by the dynamics of the family structure. Basic values and norms are encouraged by the behaviors and interactions as modeled and reinforced by those within the proximity of the family structure. An individual's affect, immediate sense of place, sense of self, and other intrinsic factors are evolved through or are the result of emotional attachment in an environment with minimal formal systems and structure. Respect for authority, the desire to accomplish tasks, and other performance characteristics are primarily attributable to factors other than those associated with satisfying a negotiated or imposed system, or an extrinsic mandate (Damon, 1990).

During this time, the family-community encourages and individuals embrace the value of belonging as well as establishing and maintaining interconnectedness to their group. Their principal spiritual evolution is grounded in the sense of belonging, identity, early attempts to establish individualism, and a rudimentary transcendental capacity bounded by the family and its managed proximity (Damon, 1990).

Cognitive Convergence

Cognitive convergence is characterized by the formal school experience wherein individuals are exposed to notions different from and frequently challenging to those they previously held. In this process, they move logically to new meanings and beliefs based on their integration of old and new. The new notions come from peers and heretofore-unknown authority figures. Systematic exposure to information and knowledge, and cognitive development through structured challenge and reinforcement of objective knowledge acquisition, moves the individual from being solely grounded in the existing emotion and beliefs to questioning the balance and disparity between these and new cognitions and to challenging what were previously almost innately accepted truths (Berkowitz, 2002; Hogg and McGary, 1990).

Although guided by structural rules, students' individualism grows and is reinforced by newly formed (albeit evolving) logic. At a spiritual dimension, the person is concerned with internal expression of being and is engaged in a quest for meaning and interconnectedness with self, others, and a higher influence (Berkowitz, 2002).

The awareness and valuing of different perspectives, the necessity of skill and knowledge acquisition as elements of personal and group success, and the valuing of those outside the family proximity for both social and task accomplishment all extend the lens through which individuals view the world and themselves in new contexts. Discovery of the self as capable of choice, willing to measure consequences of choice within the system and then act on this knowledge for the greater good, exhibits commitment to social exchange and a strong sense of affiliation commitment that reinforces self-worth. In this regard, young people experiment with building networks beyond themselves and the family proximity, thus fostering a sense of community (Fowler, 1981).

Experimental Expansion

In the postsecondary prework environment, individuals engage in broader social and intellectual experimentation and introspection. The exercise of postsecondary education engages existential capacity building by encouraging and facilitating the search for meaning and purpose in life. Research suggests that the search for meaning in life involves pursuing development of the whole person, striving for personal goals, and behaving with integrity (Helminiak, 1996; Maslow, 1971).

During this time, individuals expand their transcendental capacity by establishing relationships beyond those available to them within the constraints of previous school, community, and family structures. Such relationships typically occur on an intellectual plane and are grounded in negotiated values as well as those traditionally advanced from the social structures of their previous experiences. The environment of inquiry, behavior, and experimentation extends to the less-defined boundaries of the larger society and can include questioning and challenging existing values and constructs (Kolberg, 1981).

Authority and Spiritual Evolution

In the *formative structural evolution phase,* the principle authority figures are those defined by family roles. Authority relationships extend beyond protecting and nurturing to shaping person-to-person interactions, learning appropriate social behaviors, and accepting workplace norms. Internalization commitment is a principal manifestation of the spiritual evolution, resulting in a high level of emotional alignment with the family unit's values and beliefs without external rewards or coercion (Emmons, 1999). According to Dehler and Welsh (1994), internalization commitment brings individuals to an emotional alignment wherein they act instinctively based on the principles of their associational unit.

In the cognitive convergence phase, formal authority figures emerge from the societal structure of the K–12 classroom and other formal environments. These are dominated by a philosophy of compliance and standards. There is also an evolution of a broader peer structure, with the attendant dynamics of fit and a more implicit authority in the form of peer approval (Hogg, 2001).

From a spiritual perspective, two commitment behaviors manifest themselves. First is compliance commitment. For example, there is a de facto economic exchange between the school system and the individual around cognitive accomplishment. Effort is put forth to acquire academic acknowledgment without regard for any contribution to the system itself. Second is affiliation commitment. Achieving a sense of acceptance in nonfamily social groups stresses a social exchange that reinforces individuals' self-worth (Hogg and McGary, 1990). Geroy, Bray, and Venneberg (2005) suggest that this is a form of social capital investment characterized by interconnectedness.

In the experimental expansion phase, authority figures often exist as the result of individual choice. Unlike the early school and other formal societal structures, tertiary environments provide choice options for exposure to content and personalities. Negotiation often factors into the relationship with the authority figure, and individuals may even experiment with interpretive passive resistance to authority mandates. Generally, authority figures take a holistic view of individuals and are committed to engaging and optimizing individuals in processes that develop their sense of self and define their place in the universe (Astin and Astin, 1999).

A strong affiliation and internalization commitment is associated with individuals in this phase. Although less focused on the institution, it is strongly oriented to the abstractions of cognitively evolved values and ideals. In addition, a strong orientation to the groups represents and validates these values and ideals (Konovsky and Pugh, 1994).

Implications for Spirituality in the Workplace

Spirituality in the workplace is variously defined in the literature. Sanders, Hopkins, and Geroy (2004) summarize the most common theme of spirituality in the workplace as being the extent to which organizations encourage a sense of meaning (existential capacity building) and interconnectedness among their employees (transcendental capacity building).

Individuals have choices concerning entering, remaining in, and exiting the workplace. Kouzes and Posner (1999) note that employees look to the workplace as a medium for developing spirituality of a different sort than that grounded in a religious paradigm. Concurrently, leadership focuses on human capital efficiencies and performance optimization by managing individual development. In this managed process, individuals are moved from spiritual expression (testimony of their sense of value and belief) to expression of spirituality (their behavior dimension) in the value-laden organizational community (Craigie, 1999).

Being part of human capital has two critical dimensions. The first is the skills and knowledge needed to accomplish tasks. The evolution of a satisfactory level of compliance commitment is predicated on achieving the threshold of skills and knowledge valued by the organization. The second is the influence of an individual's intrinsic variables, such as individual spirituality on social fit and contribution to group performance and culture (Geroy and Venneberg, 2003). In these dimensions, the evolution of affiliation and internalization commitment is valued and sought from the individual by the organization.

Spiritual Self-Development Within Work Environments

Geroy, Bray, and Venneberg (2005) associate leadership behaviors within the broad community of the organization as facilitating spiritual development. The reflection of spirituality as a sense of meaning and interconnectedness, the development of the whole person, and a sense of community in the workplace advance the question, "What opportunities exist for individuals to initiate self-managed spiritual development within the context of organizational performance-managed spirituality?" Opportunities occur within three contexts of the organization's performance management spiritual dimension: coaching, counseling, and mentoring. The first occurs when individuals seek and receive authority-based *coaching* for skill development required to contribute to group accomplishment. This addresses one of the dimensions of development of the whole person. In addition, it encourages compliance commitment.

The second dimension develops when individuals seek and receive *counseling* on behaviors intended to facilitate cultural fit in the organization's social structure. This addresses dimensions of interconnectedness and sense of community, supporting the development of affiliation commitment.

Finally, the spiritual dimension matures when individuals look beyond their current station in the organization and life, seeking and receiving *mentoring* to help them transcend their current self and achieve self-actualization. Through this process, individuals evolve and transcend to a sense of meaning (Geroy, Bray, and Venneberg, 2005), sustaining internalization commitment.

Bass (1995) suggests that traits such as high self-confidence, self-determination, inner direction, and a strong conviction in the moral righteousness of his or her beliefs characterize the authority figure capable of supporting an individual's spiritual development in the organization. Research by Sanders, Hopkins, and Geroy (2004) shows that these traits may play an important role in facilitating and evolving the spiritual behavior of workers. Such traits have also been used to distinguish transactional leaders from transformational leaders (Bass, 1995).

Conclusion

Throughout the spiritual evolution of an individual (see Figure 9.1), dominant personal growth dynamics differ for each phase of individual development and maturation. Likewise, related dominant environments support these dynamics. Finally, each phase of development will have a particular structural characteristic available to facilitate spiritual development. Along this continuum, the place and role of authority, type of capacity building, and attendant commitment profiles will vary and evolve to support the individual's ability to address needs and preferences, first as a maturing individual and later as a working adult.

References

Acker, K. *Developmental Processes and Structures: Requisite to the Integration of Spirituality and Work.* Ann Arbor, Mich.: Bell and Howell—University of Michigan, 2000.

Ashmos, D. P., and Duchon, D. "Spirituality at Work: A Conceptualization and Measure." *Journal of Management Inquiry,* 2000, *9*(2), 134–145.

Astin, A. W., and Astin, H. S. *Spirituality in the Lives of College Faculty: A Study of Values, Authenticity, and Stress.* Los Angeles: Higher Education Research Institute, University of California, 1999.

Bass, B. M. "Transformational Leadership Redux." *Leadership Quarterly,* 1995, *6*(4), 463–478.

Berkowitz, M. "A Communitarian Position on Character Education." In W. Damon (ed.), *Bringing a New Era in Character Education.* Stanford, Calif.: Hoover Institutional Press, 2002.

Brandt, E. "Corporate Pioneers Explore Spirituality." *HR Magazine,* 1996, *41*(4), 83–87.

Craigie, F. C. "The Spirit and Work: Observations About Spirituality and Organizational Life." *Journal of Psychology and Christianity,* 1999, *18*(1), 43–53.

Damon, W. *The Moral Child: Nurturing Children's Natural Moral Growth.* New York: Simon & Schuster, 1990.

Dehler, G. E., and Welsh, M. A. "Spirituality and Organizational Transformation: Implications for a New Management Paradigm." *Journal of Managerial Psychology,* 1994, *9*(6), 17–26.

Emmons, R. A. *The Psychology of Ultimate Concerns: Motivation and Spirituality in Personality.* New York: Guilford Press, 1999.

Fowler, J. W. *Stages of Faith: The Psychology of Human Development and the Quest for Meaning.* San Francisco: Harper Collins, 1981.

Frankl, V. E. *Man's Search for Meaning: An Introduction to Logotherapy.* New York: Simon & Schuster, 1984.

Geroy, G. D., Bray, A., and Venneberg, D. "The CCM Model: A Management Approach to Performance Optimization." *Performance Improvement Quarterly Journal,* 2005, *18*(2), 19–36.

Geroy, G. D., and Venneberg, D. "A View to Human Capital Metrics." In A. M. Gilley, J. L. Callahan, and L. L. Bierema (eds.), *Critical Issues in HRD.* Cambridge, Mass.: Perseus, 2003.

Helminiak, D. *The Core of Spirituality: Mind as Psyche and Spirit.* Albany: State University of New York, 1996.

Hogg, M. A. "A Social Identity Theory of Leadership." *Personality and Social Psychology Review,* 2001, *5*(3), 184–200.

Hogg, M. A., and McGary, C. "Self Categorization and Social Identity." In M. A. Hogg and D. A. Abrams (eds.), *Social Identity Theory: Constructive and Critical Advances.* New York: Springer-Verlag, 1990.

Kolberg, L. The Philosophy of Moral Development: Essays on Moral Development. San Francisco: Harper & Row, 1981.

Konovsky, M. A., and Pugh, D. S. "Citizenship Behavior and Social Exchange." *Academy of Management Journal,* 1994, *37*(3), 656–669.

Kouzes, J. M., and Posner, B. Z. *Encouraging the Heart: A Leader's Guide to Rewarding and Recognizing Others.* San Francisco: Jossey-Bass, 1999.

Leigh, P. "The New Spirit at Work." *Training and Development,* 1997, *5*(3), 26–33.

Maslow, A. H. *The Farther Reaches of Human Nature.* New York: Penguin, 1971.

Mitroff, I. I., and Denton, E. A. "A Study of Spirituality in the Workplace." *Sloan Management Review,* 1999, *40*(4), 83–92.

Prehar, C. A. "Broadening Our Perspective of Employee-Organization Linkages: From Organizational Commitment to Organizational Attachment." Unpublished doctoral dissertation, Department of Psychology, Colorado State University, 2001.

Sanders, J., Hopkins, W. E., and Geroy, G. D. "Spirituality-Leadership-Commitment Relationships in the Workplace: An Exploratory Study." Paper presented at the Academy of Management Conference, New Orleans, Aug. 7, 2004.

GARY D. GEROY *is professor of human capital and economic development at Colorado State University in Fort Collins.*

10

Spirituality and service learning can be related meaningfully in institutions of higher education when there is a focus on serving others.

Spirituality and Service Learning

John Sikula, Andrew Sikula Sr.

Spirituality is the inborn desire and ability of every person to seek, to know, and to respond to God (Smith, 2001). More and more, workers want their spirituality welcomed in the workplace, just as their intelligence is (Carr, 1998). As Chittister (1995, p. 3) says, "A spirituality of work is that process by which I finally come to know that my work is God's work, unfinished by God because God meant it to be finished by me." Spirituality is also linked to preparation for work and a career (Brittan and Hamlin, 1995), and thus, increasingly, institutions of higher education are formally incorporating introspection, reflection, and practical experiences—often components of service learning—in degree programs. These components can help determine if there is a good match between students' skills and what they are preparing to do with their lives. This chapter, connecting spirituality and service learning, is timely because personal development and fulfillment are more and more the purview of higher education.

Historical Perspective

Seeing spirituality returning to higher education is refreshing. Historically, most colleges and universities in the United States and worldwide began with religious affiliations. Many started as seminaries. Courses in the Bible, religion, ethics, and philosophy were mandatory and were considered part of a general education. But spiritual slippage has evolved over the past secular decades, and today it is easy for a student to graduate with a baccalaureate degree without taking any course in religion, philosophy, or faith analysis. General education, which is the part of the curriculum where such subjects were previously taught, has been invaded more and more by vocational training. Many academicians believe that vocational and remedial education now dominates undergraduate higher education as preparation for work and has, to some degree, replaced preparation for life.

Spirituality has been reintroduced into the college curriculum during the past decade and a half, partly because people are becoming more concerned with and knowledgeable about the inadequacies of university education in preparing people to be productive citizens. Mass media have increasingly exposed hypocrisy and inconsistencies between words and actions, ivory-tower thinking and the realities of the real world. The need for closer examination of who we are as individuals, what our talents are, and what we might best contribute to society is seen as appropriate classroom content when students are in colleges and universities preparing for the future (Ridley, 1996). This preparation needs to have a strong introspective component, which can be easily associated with spirituality and with the essence of what higher education should be about.

Historically, spirituality has often been misunderstood and misapplied, being confused with cognitive thinking, which for some is indiscernible from one's physical feelings. Part of the problem is that one view of humankind is that a person is only a combined physical and mental human being (Brandt, 1997). A more accurate perspective adds a third spiritual component of human existence where the soul resides and ethics, values, and morals abound. This spiritual-mental-physical view recognizes holistic behavior where doing, thinking, and feeling are all interrelated. Healthy humans must have their physical, mental, and spiritual components in balance; each must be given some priority, and a healthy personality needs consistency in the relationships among thinking, feeling, and doing.

The 1990s marked the beginning of a new ethical-environmental era characterized by a gradual return to civility and morality (Carr, 1998). There is a slow but growing movement away from moral morass to moral management. Situational, relativistic, and contingency thinking is less acceptable today, and society has reached the limit of its willingness to permit severe deviations in thoughts, decisions, and behaviors. Society is just now beginning its moral correction and ethical readjustment. The heart and soul of this new era is a spiritual awakening and revival of worldwide proportions. Formerly atheistic countries have a built-up hunger for spiritual sustenance. In America, this spiritual awakening is less evident because freedom of religion has always been a part of the fabric of society. In America today, the religious right and political conservatives are being heard more, although they still represent a minority voice within the general public. Our new national interest in spirituality is allowing us to refocus on ideas and philosophies of the past, which were ignored or discarded by many during the materialistic and relativistic period of the 1980s.

Within the spirituality movement, an interest has been rekindled in institutions of higher education to return to more introspection and reflection in developing student potential. This spirituality movement is encouraging students to be less concerned about their own circumstances and more aware of and proactive in regard to the welfare of others as they make academic and career decisions about how they want to proceed with their work and lives (Lunati, 1997). The concept of "spirited leadership" is increasingly seen in the personnel management literature. Spirited leadership is the ability to energize and to focus the efforts of fellow human beings, resulting in a synergetic effort. Spirited leadership is inspirational and visionary, derives from personal integrity, and can help enable others to transcend existing limitations. Indeed, developing leaders involves nurturing a driving force that causes one to do the right things, as distinguished from mere managers who do things right (Bennis, 1996).

Service Learning

Learning to serve others rather than oneself does not come naturally to human beings (Waal, 1996). It has to be learned. Today, lifelong learning is being emphasized as we prepare for an unknown tomorrow, and because higher education institutions are responsible for lifelong learning, they are increasingly getting into the business and practices associated with service learning. Interest in service learning was strengthened in the 1990s by the work of several national organizations, including the American Association for Higher Education, the Council of Independent Colleges, and Campus Compact (Bringle and Hatcher, 1996).

Service learning is a method students use to learn through organized community service to care for others while earning academic credit. At many universities, service-learning opportunities, including meaningful service and structured reflection, are voluntary and can be counted for elective credit. The main difference between service learning and volunteering is that service learning involves earning credit and meeting specific educational objectives for the experience. Skills in the classroom are applied to real-life situations, and students can develop a sense of caring for others that can be used throughout their lives.

Through service learning, students can study sacred text, participate in classes and community projects, and spend time in reflection to help them understand God and their own spirituality and connectedness to society and to the world in which they live. With age, spirituality and the ability to understand and to serve others can grow and continue to unfold because we often become less self-centered with maturity and can increasingly find that our place in society involves caring for the needs of others.

Serving others has been a principle associated with many religions. For instance, the teachings of Jesus Christ can be looked to for learning how to serve others. Treating others as you yourself would want to be treated—a precept taught by Christ—has guided the lives of millions of people for centuries. Today this idea is gaining momentum in private and state–supported institutions of higher education.

Many schools, colleges, and universities today have significant experiences designed for students to learn from teachers and mentors how to serve others in their communities. Many universities allow students to design, often with the help of a professor, a community member, or both, a unique learning experience involving a community person or an organization in need. Such experiences may involve a telephone hotline for victims of domestic violence, HIV [human immunodeficiency virus]-positive persons, nursing home residents, disabled students, prisoners, homeless veterans, or any of a variety of other disadvantaged personages. Two universities that readers may want to visit online to learn how institutions of higher education can successfully implement service learning are Arizona State University (ASU) (http://www.asu.edu/duas/servicelearning) in Tempe and Cardinal Stritch University in Milwaukee, Wisconsin (http://www.stritch.edu) (Toosi, 2004).

Several universities believe that volunteerism in a minority community is indispensable in creating an improved quality of life (Carpenter and Jacobs, 1994). Among those, as noted above, is ASU, where the Service Learning Program involves teaching and tutoring academically at-risk children. ASU students at every level and in every discipline are encouraged to participate. Classroom-linked community engagement is the goal in this program that promotes students' lifelong commitment to the civic community while developing the academic skills and self-esteem of at-risk youth from preschool through K–12. The ASU program also strives to assist parents in attaining skills to act as the first teachers of their children and as mentors while developing their own self-sufficiency.

At Cardinal Stritch University and elsewhere, the focus is on finding a "calling." This can involve creating a personal wellness program that involves eating, exercising, health, recreation, and a balanced life (Guillory, 2001). Dedication is needed to develop a continuous learning program with stretch projects and coaching (Guillory, 2001). A person needs to focus thoughts and energy on the things he or she can influence or change, leaving the rest to God (Guillory, 2001). "To follow a calling may be to do what you are meant to do or be where you are supposed to be" (Goodier, 2001, p. 1). Service learning can help students discern God's will for their lives. Through service and learning, students can learn how to express workplace spirituality, providing personal support and making ethical, just decisions.

ASU and Cardinal Stritch University are preparing students for an unknown future but one in which individuals work for the survival and success of others. As is often said, university graduates in the future will have to change jobs frequently. But a constant can be serving others. Finding a calling or work that is personally satisfying is more likely to be achieved by students who engage in service–learning experiences. Research also supports the contention that service learning has a positive effect on personal, attitudinal, moral, social, and cognitive outcomes (Bringle and Hatcher, 1996).

Of course, service learning is being implemented at many other universities. Among those is Ashland University in Ashland, Ohio. However, the magnitude of the program is minimal because only 5 percent of the undergraduate student body elects to incorporate service-learning projects for elective credit toward a degree. The opportunities are developed in fewer disciplines than at ASU, and there is less emphasis than at Cardinal Stritch University to tie in the experiences with finding a "calling."

Connecting Spirituality and Service Learning

Spirituality has many definitions, and it can be seen in a variety of forms (Werhane and Freeman, 1998). Likewise, universities and colleges implement service learning differently. This is as it should be in a country as diverse as the United States of America.

The relationship between service learning and spirituality in higher education can take different manifestations that can coexist peacefully. Uniformity is not the goal. The goal is to design and implement a program that makes sense individually or locally (or both) given the history, economics, and personalities involved. Different applications can result because different situations require unique solutions for optimal results. There is no one correct way to come to know who we are, and there is no one way to learn to serve others. The complexities involved in a diverse society can be understood best by knowing and understanding how others apply the same concepts. Diversity of concept applications needs to be not only accepted but also encouraged. Differences are resources for generating wisdom, solutions, and possibilities.

Readers are encouraged to examine examples in the literature of the application of spirituality and service learning in various contexts. One resource particularly helpful in addressing the history of service learning and different theoretical models related to service learning is *Service-Learning: History, Theory, and Issues* (Speck and Hoppe, 2004). The models presented in that volume demonstrate real diversity in how service learning can be implemented. Whether one is interested in corporate America or assisting the unemployed, "The goal of service-learning should be an informed and unbiased study of social and civic issues, resulting in a commitment to participation in solving those issues for the benefit of individuals and the good of society as a whole" (Hoppe, 2004, p. 148). Another excellent resource is *Service-Learning in Higher Education* (Jacoby and Associates, 1996), which provides a comprehensive guide to developing high–quality service–learning experiences in the curriculum and through student affairs programs. Other good references include a series of paperbacks on "Service-Learning in the Disciplines" published by the American Association for Higher Education (1993). These trace historical developments associated with service learning.

As far as spirituality is concerned, innumerable references are available. Connecting spirituality directly with higher education, however, has not been commonly done—thus the need for this volume.

Conclusion

Connecting spirituality and service learning with higher education today is appropriate because higher education institutions are increasingly incorporating service learning into their operations and missions. The inclusion of spirituality has the potential to strengthen service-learning programs. Combining a national awakening of an interest in spirituality with a renewed emphasis on civic responsibility gives universities a basis for returning to more introspection and reflection in the curriculum. As part of their lifelong learning purpose, colleges and universities are paying more attention to students who are finding their callings through life experiences for credit while serving the needs of others.

References

American Association for Higher Education (AAHE). *AAHE's Series on Service-learning in the Disciplines*. Washington, D.C.: American Association for Higher Education, 1993.

Bennis, W. G. "Why Leaders Can't Lead." In J. S. Ott (ed.), *Classic Readings in Organizational Behavior*. Orlando, Fla.: Harcourt Brace, 1996.

Brandt, R. B. *Facts, Values, and Morality*. Cambridge, U.K.: Cambridge University Press, 1997.

Bringle, R. G., and Hatcher, J. A. "Implementing Service Learning in Higher Education." *Journal of Higher Education*, 1996, 67(2), 221–237.

Brittan, S., and Hamlin, A. *Market Capitalism and Moral Values*. Chelteham, U.K.: Elgar, 1995.

Carpenter, B. W., and Jacobs, J. S. "Service Learning: A New Approach in Higher Education." *Education*, 1994, 115(1), 97–99.

Carr, J. *Civil Society and Civil Society Organizations*. London: British Council, 1998.

Chittister, J. "The Spirituality of Work." Program #3913. (Dec. 31, 1995). http://www.30goodminutes.org/csec/sermon/chittister_3913.htm. Accessed Sept. 14, 2004.

Goodier, S. "Ending Up Where You Ought to Be." *Workplace Spirituality*, 2001, no page nos. [e-journal]. http://www.workplacespirituality.info/EndingWhereUOught.html. Accessed Sept. 14, 2004.

Guillory, W. "Creating a Context of Spirituality in the Workplace." *Workplace Spirituality*, 2001, no page nos. [e-journal]. http://www.workplacespirituality.info/ContextSpWorkplace.html. Accessed Sept. 12, 2004.

Hoppe, S. L. "A Synthesis of the Theoretical Stances." In B. W. Speck and S. L. Hoppe (eds.), *Service-Learning: History, Theory, and Issues*. Westport, Conn.: Praeger, 2004.

Jacoby, B., and Associates (eds.). *Service-Learning in Higher Education*. San Francisco: Jossey-Bass, 1996.

Lunati, T. M. *Ethical Issues in Economics: From Altruism to Cooperation to Equality*. London: Macmillan, 1997.

Ridley, M. *The Origins of Virtue*. London: Viking, 1996.

Smith, N. R. "What Is Workplace Spirituality?" *Workplace Spirituality*, 2001, no page nos. [e-journal]. http://www.workplacespirituality.info/article1001.html. Accessed Sept. 13, 2004.

Speck, B. W., and Hoppe, S. L. (eds.). *Service-Learning: History, Theory, and Issues.* Westport, Conn.: Praeger, 2004.

Toosi, N. "Stritch Aims to Help People from All Walks of Life Find Direction." *Milwaukee Journal Sentinel,* Jan. 8, 2004. http://jsonline.com/news/metro/janon/198370.asp. Accessed Sept. 15, 2004.

Waal, F. de. *Good Natured-The Origins of Right and Wrong in Humans and Other Animals.* Cambridge, Mass.: Harvard University Press, 1996.

Werhane, P., and Freeman, E. R. *Blackwell Encyclopedia Dictionary of Business Ethics.* Oxford, U.K.: Blackwell, 1998.

JOHN SIKULA is associate provost and dean of the Graduate School at Ashland University in Ashland, Ohio.

ANDREW SIKULA SR. is associate dean of the Lewis College of Business, director of the Graduate School of Management, and Richard G. Miller Distinguished Professor at the Marshall University Graduate College in Charleston, West Virginia.

11

*Spirit-driven leadership requires an inner journey,
wholeness, and reflection.*

Spirituality and Leadership

Sherry L. Hoppe

The twenty-first century dawned without the long-feared computer disasters legions had predicted would bring the world to its "knee chips." More quietly and much more stealthily, the new century brought a renewed interest in the polar opposite of technology: spirituality. Surely, the intellect that put zillions of bits of data onto tiny chips has discovered that the soul is really just a figment of the imagination. Indeed, an article in the September 27, 2004, edition of *Newsweek* described the brain as "a pocket PC for the soul, managing the information at the behest of a ghostly user" (Pinker, 2004, p. 78). Pinker even avows that science has now *proved* the "soul" is no more than an "information-processing activity of the brain" (p. 78).

Undoubtedly, many will rebel against findings that move the soul from the spiritual realm of the heart to the science of the brain. That may be the case even in American secular universities. After all, the earliest colleges of Colonial America honored both the intellect and the spirit, with theology holding a "foundational position, alongside the classics and the rudiments of science. . . . Education of the whole person—knowledge, talents, soul, and character—guided the enterprise, and question of ultimate meaning formed the discourse of the day" (Strange, 2004, p. 1). Only in the nineteenth century did intellect achieve preeminence, and soul was relegated to religious studies as its only proper place. Through almost all of the twentieth century, American higher education "witnessed a distinct dividing of the waters of human experience, with things of the spirit receding to one bank and things of the intellect to the other" (Strange, 2004, p. 1). In recent history, though, American higher education has seen a reawakening of an interest in spirituality. In the decade of the nineties, spirituality made its

NEW DIRECTIONS FOR TEACHING AND LEARNING, no. 104, Winter 2005 © Wiley Periodicals, Inc.

way into hundreds of books (McDonald, 1999). Interestingly, Marcic's (2000) review of approximately one hundred books and one hundred journal articles on workplace spirituality revealed that less than 20 percent mentioned God or other deity. If a higher power is not at the heart and soul of spirituality, what is?

Definitions

Defining spirituality has been the subject of many writers in recent years (Bolman and Deal, 2001; Chickering, 2004; Conger and Associates, 1994; Dalton, 2001; Fried, 2001; Hicks, 2003; Narayanasamy, 1999; Scott, 1994). Because this volume devotes an entire chapter (Chapter One) to such definitions, this chapter will not enter the debate. Instead, I note a dichotomy presented by Blanchard (1999): "We are not human beings having a spiritual experience. We are spiritual beings having a human experience" (p. 92). While this does not define spirituality, it does point out the almost inevitable outcome of any study on spirituality: more questions are asked than are answered.

For the purpose of this chapter on leadership and spirituality, I adopt a nonrestrictive definition of spirituality that allows the outcome of ongoing questions: the search for depth and meaning in our entire being. (I will use spirit and soul almost interchangeably, although some authors, including Bolman and Deal [2001], see soul as "personal and unique, grounded in the depths of personal experience" compared with the spirit as "transcendent and all embracing. . . . the universal source—and the oneness of all things" [p. 9].) As leaders, we may translate the search for depth and meaning into three questions Emmanuel Kant asserts should be asked in regard to our spiritual beliefs: "What can I know? What can I do? [and] What can I hope?" (Raper, 2001, p. 24). Dalton (2001) suggests other questions: "Why am I here? What am I meant for? What is worth living for? How can I be for myself and also for others? Whom and what do I serve? What is it that I love above all else?" (p. 17). Asking ourselves these questions sets the stage for developing leadership attributes that use not only the head and the hands but also the heart. Bolman and Deal (2001) remind us, "the heart of leadership is in the hearts of leaders" (p. 11), whereas Kurtz and Ketcham (1992) describe spirituality as transcending the ordinary "and yet, paradoxically, it can be found only in the ordinary. Spirituality is *beyond* us and yet is in everything we do. It is extraordinary, and yet it is extraordinarily simple" (p. 35). Conger and Associates (1994) cite a study by Wade Clark Roof, a religion professor, to describe what some call "heart knowledge": "'In its truest sense, spirituality gives expression to the being that is in us; it has to do with feelings, with the power that comes from within, with knowing our deepest selves and what is sacred to us . . . '" (p. 9).

Attributes of Spiritual Leadership

Accepting the premise that *asking* the questions is more important than *answering* them and that each person views the questions from his or her own frame of reference, one can still believe "Spirituality is assumed to be a dimension of the human being that is shared by all persons" (Hicks, 2003, p. 50). Consequently, all leaders will likely consider some or all of the following attributes in their quest for spiritual leadership: inner journey, meaning and significance, wholeness, and connectedness.

Inner Journey. Discovering who we are by looking deep inside ourselves sets the compass for the search for truth and meaning as individuals and as leaders. Bolman and Deal (2001) call for "classic means: an examined life, a spirit of inquiry and genuine experimentation . . . " (pp. 151–152). They purport that the "contemporary search is grounded in the age-old journey of the soul that has been a core preoccupation of every human culture since the beginning of time" (p. 4). Material success, enough for more than one generation of post-Depression Era Americans, is no longer satisfying for scores who find something elusively missing from their lives. Bolman and Deal (2001) assert that "the signs of spiritual hunger and restlessness are everywhere" and "are convinced what's really missing is soul and spirit" (p. 5). They believe that "when each of us plunges into the depths at the core of our being, there we find soul" (p. 9).

Meaning and Significance. Raper (2001) uses *The Moviegoer* to remind us that every individual would likely undertake the "search" if not "sunk in the everydayness" of life (p. 24). Those who find a way to rise above daily minutiae to try to make sense of the world and their place in it, even if the questions go unanswered, are on the path to greater understanding of self and meaning. Raper (2001) quotes Nietzsche's famous lines as proof of the reason for the quest: "'He who has a *why* to live for, can bear almost any *how*'" (p. 24). The answers within us help us overcome seemingly meaningless tragedies—not with all questions resolved but answered with a belief in who we are in the context of something more than our physical being. For leaders, that centering of oneself enables a steady course in troubled waters.

Leaders must continuously examine *why* they want to be in leadership roles. This can be accomplished in numerous ways, including reading and reflection, seminars and retreats, and daily introspection. For example, as part of an initiative for the *Journal of College and Character,* three dozen college and university presidents recorded their reflections for several years in diaries. They examined broad implications of what they were doing and how they were leading as well as what was required of them as leaders. They moved beyond the routine into self-examination, discussing how they did or did not set aside personal beliefs and values in their decision-making process (Nelson, 2002).

All leaders need to understand their motivations and their inner struggles about what is right and what is wrong. They should debate with themselves the risks of openness. And they should seek purpose for their life and work. The attribute of meaning enables spiritual leaders to "offer the gift of significance, rooted in confidence that the work is worthy of one's efforts and the institution deserves one's commitment and loyalty" (Bolman and Deal, 2003, p. 345).

Wholeness. Lives in the twenty-first century are often fragmented and individualized. As leaders, we often compartmentalize our activities, thoughts, and even values into public and private realms. Even within our public realm, we detach and isolate ourselves (especially our inner selves) from others. Bennett (2003) describes the dangers of such separation as "insistent individualism," which "views persons as detached and only externally or incidentally related to others" (p. iii). He opposes insistent individualism because of its adverse affect on faculty and staff relationships and sees evidence in "atomistic and unconnected curricula, isolated disciplines, and fragmented departments" (p. 25). He adds that insistent individualism "underwrites a philosophy of education that highlights separation; it invites the ethical charge that the academy does not practice the self-examination it preaches; and it glorifies a spirituality of self-preoccupation" (p. 25). In contrast, he suggests "relational individuality" as a healthier approach that "celebrates learning and learnedness as shared endeavors, and finds fulfillment in practicing openness to others" (p. xiv). He describes this as practicing hospitality, where confidence in self (achieved through self-examination and self-identity) enables a leader to give and receive (Bennett, 2003). That giving and receiving can transform the life of both the giver and the receiver.

How does a leader open himself or herself to giving and receiving? For some, giving is easy. It comes from an ethic in which one sees leadership as a "higher calling" (Bolman and Deal, 2001, p. 106). For others, though, neither giving nor receiving comes naturally. Bolman and Deal (2001) believe this is because many leaders rely mostly on the "rational side of enterprise" (p. 147). Separating the rational or business side of the enterprise from the spiritual dimension creates the risk of work becoming just the opportunity to make a living rather than opening the possibilities for making a difference. Bennett (2003) emphasizes that "those who make openness to others a habit seek ways to overcome the fragmentation and isolation of both individuals and institutions. They develop philosophies and ethics that promote both individual and common good. Thus they create conditions for healthy spiritualities—understandings of self as linked with others in commitments that attend to others, advance insights into self, and promote ethical fulfillment. They draw on their different strengths to pursue the common tasks of revitalizing traditions of openness—traditions that are becoming weakened and depleted as higher education becomes more a business than a social institution" (p. 185).

Spirituality thus adds a self-transcendent awareness necessary for wholeness (Greenstreet, 1999). Transcending self involves an encounter with otherness that Dalton contends is "a universal instinct toward connection with others and a discovery of our place in the larger web of life" (Dalton, 2001, p. 17).

Connectedness. The universal instinct toward connectedness described by Dalton does not match Conger's (1994) description of our tendency to "stereotype spirituality and life in organizations as opposing forces, one taking us inward to ourselves, the other taking us outward to the world" (p. xiii). However, for many of us, the place where we work has become our primary source of community. We spend more time there than any other place. We form friendships that extend beyond the workplace. And it is where we find challenge in life and an opportunity to contribute (Conger, 1994). Can we have such connectedness at work without bringing our spirituality to the workplace? Using the definition of spirituality chosen for this chapter (the search for depth and meaning in our entire being) requires connections—wherever they occur—to be a part of the wholeness, the search for meaning in all parts of our lives. This is especially important as many people try to fill the gaps created by the splintering of the extended family, the diminishing impact of rituals and traditions in churches and temples, and the growing cynicism and apathy of the civic community (Conger, 1994). In short, wholeness demands connectedness in heretofore-unexpected places in our lives, including work.

In the chaos of juggling multiple responsibilities and dealing with the often-fragmented components of our lives, Conger (1994) reminds us of the grandeur and mystery in the world and the connection among all humanity, championing the notion that "spirituality, more powerfully than most other human forces, lifts us beyond ourselves and our narrow self-interests. . . . It helps us to see our deeper connections to one another and to the world beyond ourselves" (p. 17). Those connections extend not only to others but also to historical events, to nature, to vision, and to things of the spirit (Palmer (1987). The larger reality also includes an understanding of our place in the world and beyond. For a leader, this means first connecting with one's own self before connecting with the world and its inhabitants—at work and in life at large.

Impact of Spiritual Leadership

The inner journey leads one first to a sense of self and meaning and then to an acknowledgment that connectedness is essential for wholeness in our lives. The journey leads not to a destination but to a spirit-filled life that can transform our roles as leaders. The transformation requires recognition that within our own being and throughout our connectedness, all human beings are flawed. Without this discernment, trustworthiness and compassion cannot flow freely from the leader; the absence of tolerance on the two-way street of connectedness creates dissension, and meaning is distorted. A person's ability to be tolerant of others' weaknesses and flaws is dependent on an inner compass that remains steady despite others' actions. Covey (1990) points out that "correct principles are like compasses: they are always pointing the way. And if we know how to read them, we won't get lost, confused, or fooled by conflicting voices and values. Principles are self-evident, self-validating natural laws. They don't change or shift. They provide 'true north' direction to our lives when navigating the 'streams' of our environments. Principles apply at all time in all places. They surface in the form of values, ideas, norms, and teachings that uplift, ennoble, fulfill, empower, and inspire people" (p. 19).

I believe that "true north" direction comes from a spiritual compass that includes the recognition that our flawed humanity requires forgiveness and tolerance at the very core of our brokenness. Without such a positioning within our inner being, leadership can become misguided and misdirected.

Bolman and Deal (2001) affirm the "dual messages of human imperfection and human transcendence" but maintain that "paradoxically, in accepting our imperfections, we develop the conviction needed to embark on an ill-defined search for a better place" (p. 67). They contend that denying imperfections means denying our humanity, disconnecting us from our soul. To avoid such a disconnection with its concomitant spiritual bankruptcy, leaders must recognize their own limitations and those of their followers: some based on personal experience with the history of the institution, some based on person experience outside the organization, and some just based on inherent human fallacies. Leaders must develop a tolerance for those broken by life and work, even when it means their actions are hurtful to the leader.

As a university president, I am keenly aware of the necessity for tolerance and have previously addressed the topic in a convocation speech in an attempt to mend the fences that are inevitably and continuously in need of repair between administration and faculty on most campuses. Some of what follows draws from that unpublished convocation address.

Manning (2000) wrote *The Ragamuffin Gospel* not for the "super spiritual," but for the "bedraggled, beat-up, and burnt out" (p. 15). Interestingly, followers seem to think they are the only ones who fit that description, but leaders often feel that way themselves. Perhaps we are not that way all of the time, but if we are honest, we will admit that we all are, in Manning's words, "inconsistent, unsteady *humans* whose cheese is falling off their cracker" (p. 15). Leaders, like followers, sometimes grow weary and discouraged along the way.

Quoting the French philosopher Maurice Blondel, Manning (2000) notes, "'If you really want to understand a man, don't just listen to what he says but watch what he does'" (p. 52). An Episcopal priest who lost his own compass at one time, Manning speaks from personal experience when he points out, "The dichotomy between what we say and what we do is so pervasive in the church and in society that we actually come to believe our illusions and rationalizations and clutch them to our hearts like favorite teddy bears" (p. 122). He tells us, "When I get honest, I admit I am a bundle of paradoxes. I believe and I doubt, I hope and get discouraged, I love and I hate, I feel bad about feeling good, I feel guilty about not feeling guilty. I am trusting and suspicious. I am honest and I still play games" (p. 26). If leaders are honest, do we not all have the same paradoxes within us? Can we not say to one another (in Manning's words) when others make mistakes or when they offend us, "Yes, ragamuffin, I understand. I've been there too" (p. 151)?

Manning (2000) reminds us that perhaps we should pause occasionally and realize, "Usually we see other people not as they are, but as we are. . . . If we have made peace with our flawed humanity and embraced our ragamuffin identity, we are able to tolerate in others what was previously unacceptable in ourselves. . . . Solidarity with ragamuffins frees the one who receives compassion and liberates the one who gives it in the consciousness awareness, 'I am the other'" (pp. 151, 153).

Spiritual leaders must be humble enough to acknowledge mistakes, and more importantly, we must forgive each other when mistakes are made. If we wait until our opponent—the colleague or other follower who has offended us—is good enough, moral enough, and diligent enough to be trusted, we may wait forever. And if we allow ourselves to be broken and bent by what others do, we may end up like the birches in one of Frost's poems. Frost describes the birch trees after the ice has melted from their branches,

> You may see their trunks arching in the woods
> Years afterwards, trailing their leaves on the ground
> Birches
> > —Frost ([1916] 1963)

Spirit-filled leaders, like the speaker in "Birches," sometimes

> . . . grow weary of considerations,
> And when life is too much like a pathless wood
> Where your face burns and tickles with the cobwebs
> Broken across it, and one eye is weeping
> From a twig's having lashed across it open.
> I'd like to get away from earth awhile
> And then come back to it and begin over.
> > —Frost ([1916] 1963)

For a leader, beginning over again is usually just a reaching down into the core being for renewal and strength. So the inner journey continues and is the never-ending source undergirding the sacred responsibility of relationships. Central to that responsibility is compassion. Kouzes and Posner's book *Encouraging the Heart* (1999) espouses the belief that to lead people, you have to care about them. People do not *need* encouragement. They *can* do their best without it. But it does *help* them perform at a higher level. For this reason, *Encouraging the Heart* is based on the "principles and practices that support the basic human need to be appreciated for what we do and who we are. It is about the importance of linking rewards and appreciation to standards of excellence. It's about why encouragement is absolutely essential to sustaining people's commitment to organizations and outcomes" (Kouzes and Posner, 1999, pp. xii-xiii). These authors remind us that the word *encouragement* has its root in the Latin word *cor,* which means "heart." *Courage* stems from the same root. Thus, "to have courage means to have heart" and "to encourage—to provide with or give courage—literally means to give others heart" (p. xvi).

So we return to where we began: looking for the soul and spirit in the heart instead of in the head. Within spirit-driven leadership, courage to make tough decisions and face difficult challenges comes from within as well as from the intellect or rational being. But courage has a second meaning. *Cor* also serves as the root for "cordial." Kouzes and Posner (1999) aver that encouragement is also about being charitable and generous. Leadership is thus dichotomous: "It's about toughness and tenderness. Guts and grace. Firmness and fairness. Fortitude and gratitude. Passion and compassion" (pp. xv-xvi). Bolman and Deal (2001) would add, "Love is the true hallmark of great leaders-love for their work and love for those with whom they work" (p. 108).

Bolman and Deal (2003) contend that love is absent from most organizations and institutions. Building on the work of Whitmyer (1993), they add, "Caring begins with knowing—it requires listening, understanding and accepting. It progresses through a deepened sense of appreciation, respect and, ultimately, love. Love is a willingness to reach out and open one's heart. An open heart is vulnerable. Confronting vulnerability allows us to drop our masks, meet heart to heart and be present for one another. We experience a sense of unity and delight in those voluntary, human exchanges that mold 'the soul of the community'" (p. 339).

Kouzes and Posner (1999) insist that if people work with leaders who encourage the heart, they not only will work harder but will feel better about themselves. Self-esteem goes up, and people's spirits are set free, often inspiring them to become more than they could ever have imagined. "This, indeed may be our ultimate mission as leaders" (Kouzes and Posner, 1999, pp. 11–12). Bennis (1989) sees this focus on others as a true calling and purports it is an inevitable outcome of leaders who have fully integrated lives.

Conclusion

Like Scott (1994), it is my "contention that coming to a deeper understanding of spirituality and leadership can be facilitated by an exploration of three things: the division we experience between the private and public realms of our lives, our capacity for self-knowledge, and the organizational structures in which we work and live" (p. 65). In this chapter, I have endeavored to address the first two of these and leave the remaining journey for the individual to pursue in his or her own organization.

Although the public and private dimensions of our life will always have some division, a truly spiritual person will have a wholeness through connectedness of both to the core being. Chavez (2001) speaks of spirituality as the "sense of myself as a whole, authentic, human being living in connection and communion with those around me" (p. 69). Such a life begins with an inner journey and continues with a reflective life. Contemplation is essential for leaders to have a sense of who they are, what they care about, and what they believe in—in essence, to have a bedrock in soul and spirit that gives meaning to life (Tichy and Cohen, 2003). "The Katha Upanishad describes the person who does not operate from a spiritual core as 'scattered as the rain that falls in craggy places, loses itself and becomes dispersed throughout the mountains.' In today's fast-paced world, with the rate of change increasing exponentially, ancient wisdom cautions us that we need an anchor and a place to stand that will provide stability and direction" (Allen and Kellom, 2001, p. 162). As Madame Chiang Kai-shek said in a speech during a time when it appeared that World War II would be lost, "In the end, we are all the sum total of our actions. . . . Day by day, we write our own destiny; for inexorably . . . we become what we do" (Waitley, 1983). If we lead from the spirit within us, what we become will be whole and authentic.

References

Allen, K. E., and Kellom, G. "Learning to Connect: Spirituality and Leadership." In V. W. Miller and M. M. Ryan (eds.), *Transforming Campus Life: Reflections on Spirituality and Religious Pluralism*. New York: Lang, 2001.

Bennett, J. B. *Academic Life: Hospitality, Ethics, and Spirituality*. Bolton, Mass.: Anker, 2003.

Bennis, W. *Why Leaders Can't Lead: The Unconscious Conspiracy Continues*. San Francisco: Jossey-Bass, 1989.

Blanchard, K. *The Heart of a Leader: Insights on the Art of Influence*. Escondito, Calif.: Honor Books, 1999.

Bolman, L. G., and Deal, T. E. *Leading with Soul*. San Francisco: Jossey-Bass, 2001.

Bolman, L. G., and Deal, T. E. "Reframing Ethics and Spirit." In *Business Leadership*. San Francisco: Jossey-Bass, 2003.

Chavez, A. F. "Spirit and Nature in Everyday Life: Reflections of a *Mestiza* in Higher Education." In M. A. Jablonski (ed.), *The Implications of Student Spirituality for Student Affairs Practice*. New Directions for Student Services, no. 95. San Francisco: Jossey-Bass, 2001.

Chickering, A. "Encouraging Authenticity and Spirituality in Higher Education." *College Values* [online], 2004. http://www.collegevalues.org/articles.cfm?id=1171&a=1. Accessed Sept. 20, 2004.

Conger, J. A. "Introduction: Our Search for Spiritual Community." In J. Conger and Associates (ed.), *Spirit at Work: Discovering the Spirituality in Leadership*. San Francisco: Jossey-Bass, 1994.

Conger, J. A., and Associates. "Preface." *Spirit at Work: Discovering the Spirituality in Leadership.* San Francisco: Jossey-Bass, 1994.

Covey, S. *Principle-Centered Leadership.* New York: Fireside, 1990.

Dalton, D. "Career and Calling: Finding a Place for the Spirit in Work and Community." In M. A. Jablonski (ed.), *The Implications of Student Spirituality for Student Affairs Practice.* New Directions for Student Services, no. 95. San Francisco: Jossey-Bass, 2001.

Fried, J. "Civility and Spirituality." In V. W. Miller and M. M. Ryan, (eds.), *Transforming Campus Life: Reflections on Spirituality and Religious Pluralism.* New York: Lang, 2001.

Frost, R. "Birches." *Selected Poems of Robert Frost.* Introduction by Robert Graves. New York: Holt, Rinehart and Winston, 1963. (Originally published 1916.)

Greenstreet, W. M. "Teaching Spirituality in Nursing: A Literature Review." *Nurse Education Today,* 1999, *19*, 649–658.

Hicks, D. A. *Religion and the Workplace: Pluralism, Spirituality, Leadership.* Cambridge, U.K.: Cambridge University Press, 2003.

Kouzes, J. M., and Posner, B. Z. *Encouraging the Heart: A Leader's Guide to Rewarding and Recognizing Others.* San Francisco: Jossey-Bass, 1999.

Kurtz, E., and Ketcham, K. *The Spirituality of Imperfection.* New York: Bantam, 1992.

Manning, B. *The Ragamuffin Gospel.* Sisters, Ore.: Multnomah, 2000.

Marcic, D. "God, Faith, and Management Education." *Journal of Management Education,* 2000, *24*(5), 628–649.

McDonald, M. "Shush. The Guy in the Cubicle Is Meditating." *U.S. News and World Report,* 1999, *126*(17), 46.

Narayanasamy, A. "ASSET: A Model for Actioning Spirituality and Spiritual Care Education and Training in Nursing." *Nurse Education Today,* 1999, *19*(4), 274–285.

Nelson, S. J. "Internal Journeys of College Presidents: Diary Reflections About Leader and Values: Abstract" *College Values* [online], 2002. http://www.collegevalues.org/articles.cfm?a=1&id=988. Accessed Sept. 20, 2004.]

Palmer, P. J. "Community, Conflict and Ways of Knowing: Ways to Deepen Our Educational Agenda." *Change Magazine,* Sept./Oct. 1987. Center for Teacher Formation.http://www.teacherformation.org/html/rr/community.cfm. Accessed Sept. 25, 2004.

Pinker, S. "How to Think About the Mind." *Newsweek,* Sept. 27, 2004, p. 78.

Raper, J. "Losing Our Religion: Are Students Struggling in Silence?" In V. W. Miller and M. M. Ryan (eds.), *Transforming Campus Life: Reflections on Spirituality and Religious Pluralism.* New York: Lang, 2001.

Scott, K. T. "Leadership and Spirituality: A Quest for Reconciliation." In J. Conger and Associates (eds.), *Spirit at Work: Discovering the Spirituality in Leadership.* San Francisco: Jossey-Bass, 1994.

Strange, C. "Spirituality at State: Private Journeys and Public Visions" *College Values* [online], 2000. http://www.collegevalues.org/articles.cfm?a=1&id=134. Accessed Sept. 20, 2004.

Tichy, N. M., and Cohen, E. "Why Are Leaders Important?" In *Business Leadership.* San Francisco: Jossey-Bass, 2003.

Waitley, D. *Seeds of Greatness.* Old Tappan, N.J.: Revell, 1983.

Whitmyer, C. *In the Company of Others.* New York: Putnam, 1993.

SHERRY L. HOPPE *is president of Austin Peay State University in Clarksville, Tennessee.*

12

Whereas questions about meaning and purpose are appropriate and perhaps essential in the classroom, teachers should integrate them with caution.

Whose Spirituality? Cautionary Notes About the Role of Spirituality in Higher Education

Daryl V. Gilley

> In the opening lines from "Beyond Tolerance," a performance piece presented in the fall of 1998 at the Education as Transformation National Gathering at Wellesley College, ten women move onto the stage and begin to speak:

COLBY: I am Baha'i.

ANTONIA: I am Buddhist.

DESIREE: I am Christian.

ANINDITA: I am Hindu.

LISA: I am Jain.

JACKIE: I am Jewish.

YASMEEN: I am Muslim.

SIMI: I am Sikh.

ALLAIRE: I am Unitarian Universalist.

SARAH: I am Wiccan.

COLBY: I believe in the progressive revelation of all prophets.

ANTONIA: I follow the path of Buddha.

DESIREE: Jesus is my savior.

ANINDITA: I worship Durga, Lakshmi, Saraswati, Krishna, Shiva.

LISA: I follow the teachings of Mahavirswami and the twenty-three other Thirthankars.

JACKIE: I follow the teachings of the Torah.

YASMEEN: I believe there is no God but Allah, and the prophet Mohammed, may peace be upon him, His messenger and prophet.

NEW DIRECTIONS FOR TEACHING AND LEARNING, no. 104, Winter 2005   © Wiley Periodicals, Inc.

SIMI: I believe in one God. Waheguru and the ten Gurus are my teachers.
ALLAIRE: I seek my own truth, drawing from the wisdom of all traditions.
SARAH: The Goddess is my mother [Kazanjian, 2000, p. 214. Used by permission].

In a study conducted in 2003 by Astin and Astin, 3,680 third-year students from forty-six public and private four-year U.S. colleges and universities responded to a series of questions regarding their spiritual development. Conducted by the University of California, Los Angeles's Higher Education Research Institute, the study revealed that "substantial numbers of third-year college undergraduates express a strong interest in spiritual matters" (p. 1). Responses to some of the questions provide a feeling for the importance of spirituality in the lives of these students:

• We are all spiritual beings (77 percent agree)
• Discussed religion or spirituality with friends (78 percent)
• To "some" or a "great" extent, I am searching for meaning or purpose in life (75 percent) (pp. 1–3).

With three-fourths of today's college students expressing a desire—even a need—for a deeper more meaningful existence, a life with purpose and meaning, it may be time to reconsider the role we have assumed as modern teachers, to move from the purely intellectual, rational, and logical and consider the value of embracing the mysterious.

As I begin this chapter, I make the following assumption: Whether we like it, whether we agree with it, whether we understand it, whether we are prepared for it, the fact is that most of humankind exhibits characteristics of a spiritual nature. Most of us at some point in our lives are concerned with "finding a meaningful life path" as described by Alexander (1997, p. 1) or with living lives that go "beyond the acquisition of knowledge" (Laurence, 1999, p. 14). Even though we may seldom state it as such, as human beings we desire lives that have meaning and purpose, lives that are connected to something greater than us.

If the issues raised throughout this book are indeed ones that resonate with us all, the question arises: Can we or should we ignore their importance in the lives of students? I submit that we cannot; we must not. However, we should proceed with considerable caution.

Cautionary Note One: Religion and Spirituality Are Unrelated Concepts in the Minds of Many

"Until very recently, with the exception of adult religious education, spirituality has been given little attention in mainstream academic adult education. This may be because spirituality is difficult to define and can sometimes be confused with religion" (Tisdell, 2001, p. 1).

Tisdell's observation about the difficulty of separating spirituality from religion is a point well taken and one that is made by many authors writing on the subject today. Some are concerned that things spiritual will be contaminated with religious ideas. Others raise equally passionate concerns that spirituality is the province of religion and should be accepted as such, the traditional faith systems of the world being sufficient to accommodate humankind's spiritual needs.

For better or worse, for the past four to five centuries, the accepted approach to the search for knowledge, truth, and wisdom has been through the sciences and the material world. In the United States, "Science and religion were allies at the beginning, but as the two subsequent centuries have unfolded, religion has steadily been pushed to the periphery" (Smith, 2001, p. 80). It has now been some time since the accepted path to truth, knowledge, and wisdom was through the sacred texts of the various wisdom traditions.

No doubt it is difficult to separate the concept of spirituality from religion. Whether one comes to the topic from a background steeped in religious orthodoxy or from a purely nonsectarian place, the issues of meaning-making in our lives and the lives of our students are an extremely personal and potentially explosive topic. Perhaps that is the reason spirituality or religion (or both) has remained an important but oft-ignored part of the formal instructional process.

The issue is important for another reason. Many people are so put off by the very word *religion* that unless we deal with the issue up front, we may never get to meaningful discussion. Therefore, it is important for our purpose here to choose a definition of spirituality that treats the concept as a separate and unique human attribute, realizing that most religious people also consider themselves to be spiritual but that not all spiritual people consider themselves to be religious. As English and Gillen (2000) explain, "religion is based on an organized set of principles shared by a group whereas spirituality is the expression of an individual's quest for meaning" (p. 1). Therefore, the term *spirituality* as used in these pages will be addressed on its own terms and not as a precept of faith. I choose a definition offered by Kazanjian (1998): "Spirituality in education is that which animates the mind and body, giving meaning, purpose, and context to thought, word, and action. Think of it as the meaning-making aspect of learning" (p. 38).

Cautionary Note Two: Understanding the Spirituality Issue Requires a Lot of Reading

How do we go about returning to an educational process that values meaning, relevance, and purpose as much as laws, facts, and scientific knowledge? How do we move from the one-dimensional to the multidimensional? Some in our profession are making progress in this area and have given us their recommendations and suggestions, including Palmer (1998–1999), Dirkx (1997), Gotz (1997), English and Gillen (2000), Vella (2000), and Eck (1993). I recommend them to you.

Cautionary Note Three: First Do No Harm

Let us assume that we have not been as attuned to things spiritual as we could have been. Let us assume that we make the decision to add meaning-making activities to our classrooms, to become less one-dimensional. Where do we begin, and how do we proceed?

We could follow something akin to the statement commonly but incorrectly paraphrased as the Hippocratic Oath: First, do no harm. Hippocrates actually did originate the phrase, but it was in another of his writings, Epidemics, Book I, Section I, Second Constitution ([400 B.C.] 1952, p. 46).

Remember, in higher education, we have been moving steadily away from any discussion of things spiritual for over five hundred years. We are all familiar with the more common manifestations of spirituality in a classroom setting, such as discussions centering around the question of "when bad things happen to good people." Discussing ethical issues related to the discipline or applying knowledge or skills to benefit others is also a common manifestation of spirituality entering the academy. Most teachers are familiar and even somewhat comfortable with these situations. But how do we respond when students exhibit what Dirkx (1997) calls "a continual search for meaning, a need to make sense of the changes and the empty spaces we perceive both within ourselves and our world" (p. 79)? The ill-prepared may retreat from the situation with any one of a number of excuses. A better option would be to engage the learner in an open and honest way. Three suggestions are offered, depending on the level of preparation the teacher has in his or her repertoire for dealing with issues of a spiritual nature.

First, the teacher can simply accept the situation and move on as soon as possible. In the acceptance mode, the teacher would provide a nonhostile environment for the opinion, idea, or question at hand. He or she would allow discussion of the issue without offering an opinion one way or the other. Unfortunately, this strategy would probably put a stop to any future such questions or discussion.

Second, the teacher can actively engage the moment and use it as a learning opportunity. In this approach, the teacher engages the student without feeling the need to produce or verify the correct answer. In all probability, there is no known right answer, questions of this sort having perplexed humanity for centuries. Having prepared yourself for this situation, you will know that some mysteries remain mysteries and that the student will begin to grasp that truth as well.

Third, the teacher can prepare for the moment with appropriate instructional strategies. In this approach, the teacher actively prepares to include questions of meaning in the learning process: overt, planned discourse on the truly important issues of our lives. How refreshing! Vella (2000) writes:

> Everything in your design moves toward dialogue as a plant moves toward the sunlight. Dialogue is the guiding principle. This means, however, that a teacher accepts a new role as resource person, not as expert; as guide, not as professor; as mentor, not as instructor; as educator, not as facilitator. . . . Dialogue does not mean that the educator comes in empty-handed. The substantive content he or she brings is not watered down. We design in such a way as to listen to the adult learner's experiences and knowledge base, and build on that which is known and with what is new. A final note on this topic would be to remember that silence is a very appropriate part of dialogue. Sometimes the mind needs the opportunity to reflect [p. 11].

Cautionary Note Four: Issues of the Spirit May Require More Preparation Than Those More Temporal

For the trepid, at least five mistakes should be avoided in our effort to meet the needs of the whole person. Gotz (1997, pp. 2–3) suggests five sins against the spirit that teachers must avoid:

- The abbreviation of infinity
- The capitulation to mediocrity
- The pride of reason
- The instrumentalist fallacy
- The demise of questioning

The abbreviation of infinity refers to a tendency toward partiality or fanaticism. Such an extreme orthodoxy could manifest itself in the form of political opinion, religious belief, cultural snobbery, gender bias, and so on. Holding at bay these conscious or even subconscious personal leanings to ensure an atmosphere where students truly feel that their opinions and beliefs are respected and understood is an essential first step to establishing an environment where the creative exploration of ideas can exist.

The capitulation to mediocrity refers to the tendency to default to the popular point of view just because it is the idea du jour. This "it must be right if everyone is thinking it" mentality is common among students with limited life experience. It is also sometimes found among professionals who are so knowledgeable in their specific field that they have failed to develop an appreciation and understanding for ideas outside their world that go beyond the commonplace. This capitulation to the average, the ordinary, and the commonplace does a disservice to the learners in our classrooms. Thoughts, ideas, and expressions of concern that deviate from the mainstream should be welcomed and seriously explored if the spirit of the learner is to be nurtured.

The pride of reason refers to the tendency to become so self-assured in our knowledge of a subject or discipline that we fail to see the Truth, even though we may have been searching for it for a lifetime. Those among us who have it all figured out and who propose to know all the answers are more than just a little scary. It reminds me of the comment by the writer Anne Lamont (1994) in *Bird By Bird* that "you can safely assume that you've created God in your own image when it turns out that God hates all the same people you do" (p. 22).

Succumbing to pride of reason has two distinct disadvantages. It creates an environment where personal growth ceases because there is nothing new to discover. It creates a false message to students that, first, all can be known and second, that you know it all. If they will just take notes and pay attention to your wonderful insights, they too may see the light.

The instrumentalist fallacy refers to the impact of technology on our search for truth. Students seeking answers to questions of relevance, purpose, understanding, and connection should not be distracted with the arguably impressive impact technology can have on the presentation of information. There is a time for technology in the learning experience, but not at the expense of understanding. Technology, a wonderful tool, is only a tool. The human mind is the genius in the learning process, and the minds of men and women making connection with each other in earnest consideration of important questions is an excellent first step in our search for truth.

The demise of questioning refers to the all-too-common instructional practice of the redistribution of facts or information in the guise of knowledge or wisdom. Meaningful learning, learning that goes beyond the mere attempt to help students master content, is rarely the result of the traditional lecture, laboratory exercise, or groups working together on a project, as good as these activities may be. Learning that goes beyond the superficial is marked by a caring atmosphere, supportive environment, and cognitive challenge, to paraphrase Vella (2000). Insightful, probing questions help learners to begin to know who they are and provides an opportunity to explore ideas, feelings, emotions, concepts, and attitudes on a much deeper level.

Quoting Nietzsche, Gotz (1997) raises the question of having to teach when there is nothing to say. This is perhaps more harmful to learners than no teaching at all. When there is nothing to say, ask questions.

Conclusion

The answer to the question posed in the title of this chapter, "Whose spirituality?" is both no one's and everyone's: no one's because no learner should feel ill at ease when expressing his or her personal beliefs or posing meaning-making questions because of a dogmatic or intellectually detached professor. Everyone's because every learner deserves to feel a level of comfort and confidence in the learning environment so that each can express doubts and fears without concern and expect a sympathetic and understanding ear from the teacher.

Ethics, morals, conscience, the idea of good and evil, pain and suffering, right and wrong: these and hundreds of other topics have served as catalyst to some of history's greatest minds. Contemplating them helps us to understand who we are and what we may become.

References

Alexander, H. A. "Intelligence and Passion in Teaching: Ignacio Gotz on Spirituality." In S. Laird (ed.), *Philosophy of Education Society Yearbook*. Champaign-Urbana, Ill.: Philosophy of Education Society, 1997.

Astin, A. W., and Astin, H. S. "Spirituality in College Students: Preliminary Findings from a National Study." Higher Education Research Institute, University of California, Los Angeles, 2004. http://spirituality.ucla.edu/results/Findings_2003–11–21.pdf. Accessed Oct. 12, 2004.

Dirkx, J. M. "Nurturing Soul in Adult Learning." In P. Cranton (ed.), *Transformative Learning in Action*. New Directions for Adult and Continuing Education, no. 74. San Francisco: Jossey-Bass, 1997.

Eck, D. L. *Encountering God: A Spiritual Journey from Bozeman to Banaras*. Boston: Beacon Press, 1993.

English, L., and Gillen, M. (eds.). *Addressing the Spiritual Dimensions of Adult Learning*. New Directions for Adult and Continuing Education, no. 85. San Francisco: Jossey-Bass, 2000.

Gotz, I. L. "On Spirituality and Teaching." In S. Laird (ed.), *Philosophy of Education Society Yearbook*. Champaign-Urbana, Ill.: Philosophy of Education Society, 1997.

Hippocrates. Epidemics, Book I, Section I, Second Constitution, 400 BC. In "Hippocratic Writings." *Great Books of the Western World,* Vol. 10. Chicago: Encyclopedia Britannica, 1952.

Kazanjian, V. H. "Moments of Meaning." *Connection: New England's Journal of Higher Education and Economic Development,* 1998, *13*(3), 37–39.

Kazanjian, V. H. "Beyond Tolerance: From Mono-Religious to Multi-Religious Life at Wellesley College." In V. H. Kazanjian and P. Laurence (eds.), *Education as Transformation*. New York: Lang, 2000.

Lamont, A. *Bird By Bird: Some Instructions on Writing and Life*. New York: Anchor Books, 1994.

Laurence, P. "Can Religion and Spirituality Find a Place in Higher Education?" *About Campus,* 1999, 4(5), 11–16.

Smith, H. *Why Religion Matters: The Fate of the Human Spirit in an Age of Disbelief*. New York: HarperCollins, 2001.

Tisdell, E. J. "Spirituality in Adult and Higher Education." Columbus, Ohio: ERIC Clearinghouse on Adult, Career, and Vocational Education, 2001. (ED 459 370)

Vella, J. "A Spirited Epistemology: Honoring the Adult Learner as Subject." In L. M. English and M. A. Gillen (eds.), *Addressing the Spiritual Dimensions of Adult Learning*. New Directions for Adult and Continuing Education, no 85. San Francisco: Jossey-Bass, 2000.

DARYL V. GILLEY is president of West Georgia Technical College in LaGrange, Georgia.

INDEX

Back Issue/Subscription Order Form

Copy or detach and send to:
Jossey-Bass, A Wiley Imprint, 989 Market Street, San Francisco CA 94103-1741

Call or fax toll-free: Phone 888-378-2537 6:30AM – 3PM PST; Fax 888-481-2665

Back Issues: Please send me the following issues at $29 each
(Important: please include ISBN number with your order.)

_____

_____

_____

$ _____ Total for single issues

$ _____ SHIPPING CHARGES: SURFACE Domestic Canadian

		Domestic	Canadian
First Item		$5.00	$6.00
Each Add'l Item		$3.00	$1.50

For next-day and second-day delivery rates, call the number listed above.

Subscriptions Please __ start __ renew my subscription to *New Directions for Teaching and Learning* for the year 2__ at the following rate:

U.S.	__ Individual $80	__ Institutional $170
Canada	__ Individual $80	__ Institutional $210
All Others	__ Individual $104	__ Institutional $244

Online subscriptions available too!

**For more information about online subscriptions visit
www.interscience.wiley.com**

$ _____ Total single issues and subscriptions (Add appropriate sales tax for your state for single issue orders. No sales tax for U.S. subscriptions. Canadian residents, add GST for subscriptions and single issues.)

__Payment enclosed (U.S. check or money order only)
__VISA __ MC __ AmEx #_____ Exp. Date _____

Signature _____ Day Phone _____
__ Bill Me (U.S. institutional orders only. Purchase order required.)

Purchase order # _____
Federal Tax ID13559302   **GST 89102 8052**

Name _____

Address _____

_____

Phone _____ E-mail _____

For more information about Jossey-Bass, visit our Web site at www.josseybass.com

TL98 Decoding the Disciplines: Helping Students Learn Disciplinary Ways of Thinking
David Pace, Joan Middendorf
The Decoding the Disciplines model is a way to teach students the critical-thinking skills required to understand their specific discipline. Faculy define bottlenecks to learning, dissect the ways experts deal with the problematic issues, and invent ways to model experts' thinking for students. Chapters are written by faculty in diverse fields who successfully used these methods and became involved in the scholarship of teaching and learning.
ISBN: 0-7879-7789-6

TL97 Building Faculty Learning Communities
Milton D. Cox, Laurie Richlin
A very effective way to address institutional challenges is a faculty learning community. FLCs are useful for preparing future faculty, reinvigorating senior faculty, and implementing new courses, curricula, or campus initiatives. The results of FLCs parallel those of student learning communities, such as retention, deeper learning, respect for others, and greater civic participation. This volume describe FLCs from a practitioner's perspective, with plenty of advice, wisdom, and lessons for starting your own FLC.
ISBN: 0-7879-7568-0

TL96 Online Student Ratings of Instruction
Trav D. Johnson, D. Lynn Sorenson
Many institutions are adopting Web-based student ratings of instruction, or are considering doing it, because online systems have the potential to save time and money among other benefits. But they also present a number of challenges. The authors of this volume have firsthand experience with electronic ratings of instruction. They identify the advantages, consider costs and benefits, explain their solutions, and provide recommendations on how to facilitate online ratings.
ISBN: 0-7879-7262-2

TL95 Problem-Based Learning in the Information Age
Dave S. Knowlton, David C. Sharp
Provides information about theories and practices associated with problem-based learning, a pedagogy that allows students to become more engaged in their own education by actively interpreting information. Today's professors are adopting problem-based learning across all disciplines to facilitate a broader, modern definition of what it means to learn. Authors provide practical experience about designing useful problems, creating conducive learning environments, facilitating students' activities, and assessing students' efforts at problem solving.
ISBN: 0-7879-7172-3

TL94 Technology: Taking the Distance out of Learning
Margit Misangyi Watts
This volume addresses the possibilities and challenges of computer technology in higher education. The contributors examine the pressures to use technology, the reasons not to, the benefits of it, the feeling of being a learner as well as a teacher, the role of distance education, and the place of computers in the modern world. Rather than discussing only specific successes or failures, this issue addresses computers as a new cultural symbol and begins meaningful conversations about technology in general and how it affects education in particular.
ISBN: 0-7879-6989-3

NEW DIRECTIONS FOR TEACHING AND LEARNING IS NOW AVAILABLE ONLINE AT WILEY INTERSCIENCE

What is Wiley InterScience?

Wiley InterScience is the dynamic online content service from John Wiley & Sons delivering the full text of over 300 leading scientific, technical, medical, and professional journals, plus major reference works, the acclaimed Current Protocols laboratory manuals, and even the full text of select Wiley print books online.

What are some special features of Wiley InterScience?

Wiley Interscience Alerts is a service that delivers table of contents via e-mail for any journal available on Wiley InterScience as soon as a new issue is published online.
EarlyView is Wiley's exclusive service presenting individual articles online as soon as they are ready, even before the release of the compiled print issue. These articles are complete, peer-reviewed, and citable.
CrossRef is the innovative multi-publisher reference linking system enabling readers to move seamlessly from a reference in a journal article to the cited publication, typically located on a different server and published by a different publisher.

How can I access Wiley InterScience?

Visit http://www.interscience.wiley.com.

Guest Users can browse Wiley InterScience for unrestricted access to journal tables of contents and article abstracts, or use the powerful search engine.
Registered Users are provided with a *Personal Home Page* to store and manage customized alerts, searches, and links to favorite journals and articles. Additionally, Registered Users can view free online sample issues and preview selected material from major reference works.
Licensed Customers are entitled to access full-text journal articles in PDF, with select journals also offering full-text HTML.

How do I become an Authorized User?

Authorized Users are individuals authorized by a paying Customer to have access to the journals in Wiley InterScience. For example, a university that subscribes to Wiley journals is considered to be the Customer.
Faculty, staff and students authorized by the university to have access to those journals in Wiley InterScience are Authorized Users. Users should contact their library for information on which Wiley journals they have access to in Wiley InterScience.

United States Postal Service

Statement of Ownership, Management, and Circulation

1. Publication Title	2. Publication Number	3. Filing Date
New Directions For Teaching And Learning	0 2 7 1 – 0 6 3 3	10/1/05

4. Issue Frequency	5. Number of Issues Published Annually	6. Annual Subscription Price
Quarterly	4	$180.00

7. Complete Mailing Address of Known Office of Publication (Not printer) (Street, city, county, state, and ZIP+4)

Wiley Subscription Services, Inc. at Jossey-Bass, 989 Market Street, San Francisco, CA 94103

Contact Person: Joe Schuman
Telephone: (415) 782-3232

8. Complete Mailing Address of Headquarters or General Business Office of Publisher (Not printer)

Wiley Subscription Services, Inc., 111 River Street, Hoboken, NJ 07030

9. Full Names and Complete Mailing Addresses of Publisher, Editor, and Managing Editor (Do not leave blank)

Publisher (Name and complete mailing address)

Wiley, San Francisco, 989 Market Street, San Francisco, CA 94103-1741

Editor (Name and complete mailing address)

Marilla D. Svinicki, Center for Teaching Effectiveness/Univ. of Austin, Main Bldg. 2200, Austin, Tx 78712-1111

Managing Editor (Name and complete mailing address)

None

10. Owner (Do not leave blank. If the publication is owned by a corporation, give the name and address of the corporation immediately followed by the names and addresses of all stockholders owning or holding 1 percent or more of the total amount of stock. If not owned by a corporation, give the names and addresses of the individual owners. If owned by a partnership or other unincorporated firm, give its name and address as well as those of each individual owner. If the publication is published by a nonprofit organization, give its name and address.)

Full Name	Complete Mailing Address
Wiley Subscription Services, Inc.	111 River Street, Hoboken, NJ 07030
(see attached list)	

11. Known Bondholders, Mortgagees, and Other Security Holders Owning or Holding 1 Percent or More of Total Amount of Bonds, Mortgages, or Other Securities. If none, check box. ▶ ☑ None

Full Name	Complete Mailing Address
None	

12. Tax Status (For completion by nonprofit organizations authorized to mail at nonprofit rates) (Check one)
The purpose, function, and nonprofit status of this organization and the exempt status for federal income tax purposes:
☐ Has Not Changed During Preceding 12 Months
☐ Has Changed During Preceding 12 Months (Publisher must submit explanation of change with this statement)

PS Form 3526, October 1999 (See Instructions on Reverse)

13. Publication Title	14. Issue Date for Circulation Data Below
New Directions For Teaching And Learning	Summer 2005

15.	Extent and Nature of Circulation	Average No. Copies Each Issue During Preceding 12 Months	No. Copies of Single Issue Published Nearest to Filing Date
a.	Total Number of Copies (Net press run)	2004	1886
b. Paid and/or Requested Circulation	(1) Paid/Requested Outside-County Mail Subscriptions Stated on Form 3541. (Include advertiser's proof and exchange copies)	936	854
	(2) Paid In-County Subscriptions Stated on Form 3541 (Include advertiser's proof and exchange copies)	0	0
	(3) Sales Through Dealers and Carriers, Street Vendors, Counter Sales, and Other Non-USPS Paid Distribution	0	0
	(4) Other Classes Mailed Through the USPS	0	0
c.	Total Paid and/or Requested Circulation [Sum of 15b. (1), (2),(3),and (4)] ▶	936	854
d. Free Distribution by Mail (Samples, complimentary, and other free)	(1) Outside-County as Stated on Form 3541	0	0
	(2) In-County as Stated on Form 3541	0	0
	(3) Other Classes Mailed Through the USPS	0	0
e.	Free Distribution Outside the Mail (Carriers or other means)	37	35
f.	Total Free Distribution (Sum of 15d. and 15e.) ▶	37	35
g.	Total Distribution (Sum of 15c. and 15f) ▶	973	889
h.	Copies not Distributed	1031	997
i.	Total (Sum of 15g. and h.) ▶	1031	1886
j.	Percent Paid and/or Requested Circulation (15c. divided by 15g. times 100)	96%	96%

16. Publication of Statement of Ownership
☑ Publication required. Will be printed in the Winter 2005 issue of this publication. ☐ Publication not required.

17. Signature and Title of Editor, Publisher, Business Manager, or Owner

Susan E. Lewis, VP & Publisher - Periodicals

Date: 10/01/05

I certify that all information furnished on this form is true and complete. I understand that anyone who furnishes false or misleading information on this form or who omits material or information requested on the form may be subject to criminal sanctions (including fines and imprisonment) and/or civil sanctions (including civil penalties).

Instructions to Publishers

1. Complete and file one copy of this form with your postmaster annually on or before October 1. Keep a copy of the completed form for your records.

2. In cases where the stockholder or security holder is a trustee, include in items 10 and 11 the name of the person or corporation for whom the trustee is acting. Also include the names and addresses of individuals who are stockholders who own or hold 1 percent or more of the total amount of bonds, mortgages, or other securities of the publishing corporation. In item 11, if none, check the box. Use blank sheets if more space is required.

3. Be sure to furnish all circulation information called for in item 15. Free circulation must be shown in items 15d, e, and f.

4. Item 15h., Copies not Distributed, must include (1) newsstand copies originally stated on Form 3541, and returned to the publisher, (2) estimated returns from news agents, and (3), copies for office use, leftovers, spoiled, and all other copies not distributed.

5. If the publication had Periodicals authorization as a general or requester publication, this Statement of Ownership, Management, and Circulation must be published; it must be printed in any issue in October or, if the publication is not published during October, the first issue printed after October.

6. In item 16, indicate the date of the issue in which this Statement of Ownership will be published.

7. Item 17 must be signed.

Failure to file or publish a statement of ownership may lead to suspension of Periodicals authorization.

PS Form 3526, October 1999 (Reverse)